Teste Dein Englisch!

Stufe 3

Ein Testbuch für Könner

Von
Geoffrey Broughton

Langenscheidt

Berlin · München · Wien · Zürich · New York

Neben den drei Bänden von TESTE DEIN ENGLISCH!
liegt im gleichen Verlag auch der Band
TESTE DEIN BUSINESS ENGLISH! vor
(ISBN 3-468-38503-X).
Mit diesem Band können Sie Ihre Kenntnisse in der
englischen Wirtschaftssprache verbessern.

Auflage:	16.	15.	14.	13.	Letzte Zahlen
Jahr:	1999	98	97	96	maßgeblich

Originalausgabe: "Know Your English", Hutchinson & Co
(Publishers) Ltd, London

Zeichnungen: Derek Alder
Umschlagentwurf: grafik-dienst
Druck: Presse-Druck Augsburg
Printed in Germany · ISBN 3-468-38502-1

Zur Einführung

Alle Anfänger und viele Fortgeschrittene machen Fehler, die ihre englischsprechenden Partner als merkwürdig, komisch oder peinlich empfinden. Sie gebrauchen das falsche Wort, die falsche Wendung, eine falsche grammatische Form oder eine unkorrekte Aussprache. Mit TESTE DEIN ENGLISCH! bekommt der Englischlernende solche Dinge in den Griff. Seine Englischkenntnisse werden durch Abtesten systematisch aufgebaut.

Das Testprinzip dieses Buches ist das „Multiple-choice-Verfahren", d. h. nach jeder in Englisch gestellten Frage werden dem Lernenden 5 Antworten zur Auswahl angeboten, von denen er eine als die richtige Lösung kennzeichnen muß. Durch Umblättern zu den „Answers" kann er sich dann selbst kontrollieren; er findet dort auch die Begründung für die richtige Lösung sowie weitere Erläuterungen zum Fragenkomplex.

Diese Methode unterscheidet sich von den herkömmlichen Lernformen. Sie ist anregend, oft amüsant. Die Kürze der Lerneinheit – die Frage – ermöglicht ein zwangloses Arbeiten auch unterwegs oder wenn wenig Zeit zur Verfügung steht.

Trotzdem basiert die Methode auf modernen linguistischen Erkenntnissen. Dafür bürgt schon der Name des Autors. Geoffrey Broughton ist Leiter des „Department of English as a Foreign Language" an der Londoner Universität. Seine erfolgreichen Lehrbücher sind in der ganzen Welt verbreitet. Aus eigener Praxis kennt er die Fallen, welche die englische Sprache für den Lernenden bereithält.

Die Serie TESTE DEIN ENGLISCH! umfaßt drei Bände, die nach Schwierigkeitsstufen gegliedert sind:

Stufe 1 – ein Testbuch für Anfänger
Stufe 2 – ein Testbuch für Fortgeschrittene
Stufe 3 – ein Testbuch für Könner

Wenn Sie nur geringe Englischkenntnisse haben, beginnen Sie mit dem Band der Stufe 1. Stufe 2 ist für denjenigen gedacht, der schon einige Jahre Englisch gelernt hat. Falls Sie sich aber als „Könner" betrachten, dann zeigt Ihnen Stufe 3, daß es auch für Sie noch einige „harte Nüsse" gibt.

So arbeiten Sie mit diesem Buch

- Nach dem Lesen jeder Frage prüfen Sie bitte sorgfältig, welche der nachgestellten 5 Antworten (a–e) die richtige Lösung darstellt.

- Wenn Sie die richtige Antwort gefunden haben, schreiben Sie den entsprechenden Buchstaben (a, b, c, d, e) in das Kästchen am Rand.

- Haben Sie eine Unit durchgearbeitet, so schlagen Sie die „Answers" auf. Prüfen Sie jetzt, ob Ihre Antworten richtig waren, und studieren Sie die Erläuterungen zu den Fragenkomplexen.

- Ermitteln Sie die Anzahl Ihrer richtigen Antworten und tragen Sie das Ergebnis in das Kästchen für die betreffende Unit auf der Seite „Ihr Testergebnis" ein.

- Auf den Seiten „Wie geht es weiter?" am Ende von Teil A und B werden Ihre Testergebnisse ausgewertet und danach die Weichen für Ihre weitere Arbeit gestellt.

- Das INHALTSVERZEICHNIS finden Sie auf Seite 224.

TEIL A

Unit one

1 All these words mean *rude*, but which is the strongest?

a. ill-mannered
b. impolite
c. insolent
d. discourteous
e. uncivil

2 An American says *suspenders* when an Englishman says

a. braces
b. garters
c. belts
d. suspenders
e. girdles

3 What is a turntable?

a. a traitor
b. the part of a record player which carries the record
c. a machine for making table legs
d. a folding table
e. a roulette wheel

4 If someone is not likely to pass an examination, we say his chances are

a. frail
b. weak
c. slim
d. sickly
e. faint

5 Which of these means something different from the others?
a. an unmistakable Picasso
b. a genuine Picasso
c. an actual Picasso
d. a veritable Picasso
e. an authentic Picasso

6 This man is using
a. a support
b. a prop
c. a crutch
d. a stand
e. a walking stick

7 Complete this phrase: as fit as
a. a violin
b. a cello
c. a fiddle
d. a harp
e. a double bass

8 A person who helps you to break the law is
a. a partner
b. an aide
c. an ally
d. an accomplice
e. a collaborator

9 *To stir* means *to make something move,* but which of these is wrong?
a. The wind stirred the leaves.
b. The cook stirred the soup.
c. The chauffeur stirred the engine.
d. The story stirred his imagination.
e. He didn't stir a muscle.

10 Which of these means *to make a guess*?
a. to submit a guess
b. to propound a guess
c. to propose a guess
d. to hazard a guess
e. to suggest a guess

11 Which of these is wrong?
a. a branch of a tree
b. a branch of a meal
c. a branch of a river
d. a branch of a railway line
e. a branch of a family

12 If you leave someone high and dry, you leave him
a. drunk
b. sober
c. stranded
d. in safety
e. thirsty

13 Finish this proverb: One man's . . . is another man's poison.
a. meat
b. nourishment
c. victuals
d. grub
e. fodder

14 Which of these can describe a tall man?
a. high
b. elevated
c. exalted
d. lofty
e. lanky

15 If a driver knocks down a pedestrian and then does not stop, it is a . . . accident.

a. hit or miss
b. hit and run
c. hit and drive
d. hit and escape
e. hit and run over

16 A large shop is divided into

a. classes
b. departments
c. categories
d. divisions
e. sections

17 What would you use to find out exactly where Copenhagen is?

a. a directory
b. a dictionary
c. a timetable
d. an atlas
e. a biography

18 Which phrase goes with the picture?

a. setting the pace
b. setting sail
c. setting his house in order
d. setting out
e. setting the fashion

19 The words *vice*, *plane* and *mallet* all have something to do with

a. sin
b. woodwork
c. travel
d. punishment
e. police

20 *To lose face* means

a. to lose consciousness
b. to be humiliated
c. to lose your good looks
d. to look vacant
e. to remove make-up from your face

Unit two

1 All children in Britain know the song: Baa, baa, black sheep, have you any

a. wool
b. white sheep
c. friends
d. grass
e. lambs

2 Which of these words is nearest in meaning to *polite*?

a. cultivated
b. refined
c. courteous
d. gallant
e. polished

3 Complete this phrase: as bold as
- a. bronze
- b. brass
- c. copper
- d. steel
- e. aluminium

4 If you turn a blind eye to something, you
- a. ignore it
- b. are blind in one eye
- c. are going round a blind corner
- d. have a black eye
- e. cannot judge it

5 Which man is not necessarily in a boat?
- a. He's rowing.
- b. He's sailing.
- c. He's canoeing.
- d. He's paddling.
- e. He's sculling.

6 Which of these is wrong?
- a. He booked in.
- b. He booked down.
- c. He is booked up.
- d. He booked the seats.
- e. He was booked.

7 The top of your head is called your
- a. crest
- b. crown
- c. summit
- d. peak
- e. apex

8 When two colours go with each other, we say they

a. match
b. suit
c. accord
d. correspond
e. tally

9 An American says *an apartment* when an Englishman says

a. a flat
b. a house
c. a villa
d. a mansion
e. a bungalow

10 Four of these sports take place on horseback: which does not?

a. fox-hunting
b. surfing
c. point-to-point
d. show-jumping
e. steeplechasing

11 Which phrase goes with the picture?

a. following the score
b. settling old scores
c. the half-time score
d. scores of times
e. on more than one score

12 Another word for *a drinking glass* is
a. a tumbler
b. a cruet
c. a decanter
d. a punch bowl
e. a tureen

13 Complete this sentence: I must have all the facts and
a. details
b. numbers
c. accounts
d. calculations
e. figures

14 When the weather man says what the weather will be like tomorrow, he is giving
a. a prophecy
b. a premonition
c. a forecast
d. a prediction
e. anticipation

15 Another word for *numb* is
a. insensitive
b. painless
c. senseless
d. unfeeling
e. nonsensical

16 You cross from the land onto a ship by
a. a bridge
b. a pontoon
c. a gangway
d. a drawbridge
e. a catwalk

17 What does the temperature do when it becomes colder?
a. shrink
b. shrivel
c. diminish
d. contract
e. decrease

18 Which phrase goes with the picture?
a. breaking the ice
b. breaking the news
c. breaking out
d. breaking her word
e. breaking down

19 Which of these is wrong?
a. in a hurry
b. in a rush
c. in a haste
d. in a scramble
e. in a flap

20 All these mean *to walk unsteadily* or *uncertainly*. Which one can also mean *to speak uncertainly*?
a. to falter
b. to limp
c. to hobble
d. to totter
e. to stagger

Unit three

1 *Proper* is to *improper* as *pure* is to
a. mispure
b. inpure
c. impure
d. dispure
e. nonpure

2 The words *span, suspension* and *cantilever* all have something to do with
a. bicycles
b. the hand
c. chemistry
d. time
e. bridges

3 Which of these can you not apply for?
a. a job
b. an appointment
c. a position
d. a post
e. a career

4 A cock and bull story is
a. a fable
b. a parable
c. a funny story
d. an anecdote
e. an incredible story

5 Which of these pipes or passages carries smoke or hot air?
a. a flue
b. a channel
c. a main
d. an artery
e. a hose

6 What did Little Bo-peep lose?
a. a keep
b. her sweep
c. a heap
d. her sleep
e. her sheep

7 Complete this phrase: as cool as
a. an iceberg
b. a marrow
c. a snowdrift
d. a pool
e. a cucumber

8 A fisherman uses
a. appliances
b. instruments
c. equipment
d. apparatus
e. tackle

9 Which phrase goes with the picture?
a. on his round
b. a round of toast
c. a round number
d. a round of drinks
e. a roundabout

10 Two people talking very frankly to each other are having a man . . . man talk.

a. with
b. before
c. against
d. to
e. at

11 An American talks about *checkers* when an Englishman says

a. draughts
b. chess
c. dominoes
d. dice
e. poker

12 The place where a river starts is its

a. beginning
b. outset
c. origin
d. introduction
e. source

13 What is the difference between cancelling a football match and postponing it?

a. They mean the same and the match is put off until a later date.
b. They mean the same and the match is put off for ever.
c. *To cancel* means to put off to a later date and *to postpone* means to put off for ever.
d. *To postpone* means to put off to a later date and *to cancel* means to put off for ever.
e. They both mean that the time is changed but not the day.

14 Which of these is nearest in meaning to *a quest*?
a. a search
b. a question
c. a query
d. an inquiry
e. an inquest

15 Which of these is wrong?
a. a bill of fare
b. a bill of sale
c. a bill sticker
d. a bill bird
e. a clean bill of health

16 Which word would you not use to describe a jewel?
a. priceless
b. costly
c. expensive
d. precious
e. dear

17 Which of these goes with the picture?
a. a tip-off
b. on the tip of your tongue
c. to leave a tip
d. on tip-toe
e. a rubbish tip

18 Finish this proverb: A bird in the hand is worth two in the

a. tree
b. wood
c. shrubbery
d. bush
e. forest

19 All these describe things you do not like. Which cannot be used of a person?

a. intolerable
b. unbearable
c. unpalatable
d. insufferable
e. unendurable

20 Which of these is wrong?

a. a flimsy difference
b. a trivial difference
c. a trifling difference
d. a slight difference
e. a minute difference

Unit four

1 Finish this line from a well-known nursery rhyme: Sing a song of sixpence, a pocket full of

a. corn
b. rye
c. barley
d. wheat
e. oats

2 The centre part of a wheel is called the

a. heart
b. hub
c. nucleus
d. core
e. focus

3 All these are shades of red: which is the darkest?

a. maroon
b. rose
c. scarlet
d. crimson
e. pink

4 If you tell a small child to *go bye-byes*, where is he going?

a. to the park
b. for a walk
c. home
d. to school
e. to sleep

5 If you never save any money, you live from hand to

a. pocket
b. purse
c. hunger
d. poverty
e. mouth

6 Finish this phrase: as easy as

a. forty winks
b. dropping off
c. closing your eyes
d. winking
e. blinking

7 Which of these is the most formal?

a. a talk
b. an interview
c. a chat
d. a conversation
e. a discussion

8 Which of these is wrong?

a. a bell push
b. a bell ringer
c. a bell tent
d. a bell tapper
e. a bell tower

9 *To stand on your own feet* means

a. to stand on tip-toe
b. to be clumsy
c. to be safe
d. to be independent
e. to stand up

10 An American talks about *a deck* of cards when an Englishman says

a. a set of cards
b. a hand of cards
c. a stack of cards
d. a packet of cards
e. a pack of cards

11 Finish this proverb: Once bitten, twice

a. diffident
b. shy
c. timid
d. reserved
e. coy

12 If someone tells you that you look under the weather, he means

a. you look rather unwell
b. your hair is windblown
c. your face is weatherbeaten
d. you are suntanned
e. you look cold

13 This woman is
a. soaked to the skin
b. soaked to the flesh
c. soaked to the bones
d. soaked to the through
e. soaked to the skeleton

14 Which of these suggests conceit?
a. to show off
b. to demonstrate
c. to show
d. to exhibit
e. to display

15 If you hear of the late Mr Jones, you know he is
a. dead
b. usually late
c. late on this occasion
d. sometimes late
e. now Lord Jones

16 Which of these cannot dissolve?
a. sugar
b. salt
c. a marriage
d. Parliament
e. a theatre play

17 Which of these is wrong?
a. He launched his head back.
b. He flung his head back.
c. He threw his head back.
d. He cast his head back.
e. He tossed his head back.

18 You would describe a very small sound as

a. weak
b. shaky
c. faint
d. limp
e. frail

19 Which phrase goes with the picture?

a. the jet set
b. a set square
c. on set
d. a set-to
e. a portable set

20 If you take off your clothes and put on different ones, you have

a. altered
b. modified
c. varied
d. changed
e. recast

Unit five

1 If you write to the person who is living in a house, but you do not know his name, you address the letter to the
a. resident
b. population
c. inhabitant
d. dweller
e. occupier

2 Which of these has a different meaning from the others?
a. He put out his hand.
b. He reached out his hand.
c. He stretched out his hand.
d. He extended his hand.
e. He spread out his hand.

3 Complete this phrase: as flat as
a. an omelette
b. a wafer
c. a pancake
d. a biscuit
e. a doughnut

4 Which word cannot complete the following sentence? I'm tired of this . . . rain.
a. infinite
b. continual
c. eternal
d. perpetual
e. continuous

5 An American talks about *a janitor* when an Englishman says
a. a cleaner
b. a porter
c. a guard
d. a watchman
e. a caretaker

6 Choose the word which describes all the others.
a. shoot
b. behead
c. hang
d. electrocute
e. execute

7 This statue is on
a. a support
b. a prop
c. a pillar
d. a plinth
e. a shaft

8 If you take a dim view of something, you
a. are going blind
b. disapprove of it
c. are short-sighted
d. are long-sighted
e. are wearing sunglasses

9 Which of these is wrong?
a. an identity card
b. an identity disc
c. an identity parade
d. an identity person
e. mistaken identity

10 Finish this proverb: Every cloud has a silver

a. interior
b. middle
c. centre
d. lining
e. inside

11 When people have a party to meet after a long time, it is

a. an entertainment
b. a reunion
c. a festival
d. a festivity
e. a reception

12 A car broken down in the middle of the road is

a. an obstacle
b. a hindrance
c. an obstruction
d. an impediment
e. an inhibition

13 The time between day and night is called

a. gloom
b. dimness
c. dusk
d. obscurity
e. darkness

14 Which speaker is not going to pay any money?

a. I'll pay the bill.
b. I'll settle the account.
c. I'll defray the expenses.
d. I'll answer the charge.
e. I'll cover the cost.

15 Which word means *to separate carefully in order to study*?
a. to divorce
b. to share out
c. to divide
d. to split
e. to dissect

16 Which is the strongest?
a. delight
b. happiness
c. ecstasy
d. pleasure
e. joy

17 *Brush* means all of these except one.
a. a fox's tail
b. undergrowth
c. a mass of thick, untidy hair
d. a short, sharp fight
e. something to sweep the floor with

18 The water in your mouth is called
a. mouthwash
b. dribble
c. sweat
d. perspiration
e. saliva

19 Which phrase goes with the picture?
a. armed to the teeth
b. by the skin of his teeth
c. a sweet tooth
d. fighting tooth and nail
e. long in the tooth

20 Which of these is wrong?
   a. He blew the trouble up.
   b. He blew up the tyre.
   c. A storm blew up.
   d. He blew up.
   e. The house blew up.

Unit six

---

1 All these words mean *raining*: which is the right order, starting with the lightest rain?
   a. pouring, drizzling, spitting
   b. drizzling, spitting, pouring
   c. spitting, pouring, drizzling
   d. drizzling, pouring, spitting
   e. spitting, drizzling, pouring

2 Another way of saying *most certainly* is *without . . . of a doubt*.
   a. a shadow
   b. a portion
   c. a crumb
   d. a piece
   e. a bit

3 All of these mean *a hole in the ground*: which of them could be called *a tunnel*?
   a. a hollow
   b. a pit
   c. a cavern
   d. a burrow
   e. an excavation

4 Instead of saying *I met a friend*, you could say
a. I joined a friend.
b. I coincided with a friend.
c. I touched a friend.
d. I encountered a friend.
e. I contacted a friend.

5 Which speaker has discovered something?
a. I came up to the house.
b. I came round the house.
c. I came across the house.
d. I came for the house.
e. I came by the house.

6 Complete this phrase: as fresh as
a. a marigold
b. a wallflower
c. a buttercup
d. a daisy
e. a poppy

7 When no rain falls for a very long time, there may be
a. a famine
b. a dearth
c. a drought
d. a deficiency
e. a scarcity

8 In a court of law, the jury reaches
a. a decision
b. a verdict
c. a judgement
d. a conclusion
e. an assessment

9 Which phrase goes with the picture?
a. red tape
b. to roll out the red carpet
c. a red rag to a bull
d. caught red-handed
e. a red herring

10 All these words mean *to hold* in a certain way. Which word means *to hold lovingly and closely with both arms*?
a. to grip
b. to clutch
c. to embrace
d. to grasp
e. to clinch

11 When a train does not arrive at the proper time at the station, the announcer apologises because it is
a. retarded
b. delayed
c. tardy
d. belated
e. overdue

12 Finish this proverb: . . . is the mother of invention.
a. Lack
b. Want
c. Defect
d. Necessity
e. Need

13 The first musician of a band or orchestra is
a. the chief
b. the head
c. the king
d. the master
e. the leader

14 An American says *a drugstore* when an Englishman says
a. a grocer's
b. a greengrocer's
c. a doctor's
d. a chemist's
e. a butcher's

15 Which of these is not a butt?
a. a large barrel
b. the handle of a sword
c. the wooden end of a rifle
d. the unburnt end of a cigarette
e. a sharp push with the head

16 Which phrase goes with the picture?
a. letting him off
b. letting the cat out of the bag
c. letting him down
d. letting sleeping dogs lie
e. letting his hair down

17 The line which a plough cuts in the ground is

a. a furrow
b. a valley
c. a trench
d. a trough
e. a vale

18 When people are angry they often . . . their teeth.

a. tighten
b. clench
c. screw up
d. curl
e. purse

19 Which is the strongest?

a. wretched
b. miserable
c. unhappy
d. woebegone
e. cheerless

20 Another way of saying *the whole day long* is

a. from dawn to evening
b. from dawn to sunset
c. from dawn to dusk
d. from dawn to twilight
e. from dawn to sundown

Unit seven

1 What does P.T.O. mean?
- a. Police Transport Organisation
- b. Public Transport Office
- c. Please turn over
- d. Potatoes, turnips and onions
- e. Pay to order

2 Finish this phrase: as sound as
- a. a chime
- b. a tambourine
- c. a bell
- d. a gong
- e. a drum

3 Which of these containers is not necessarily round?
- a. a barrel
- b. a bin
- c. a drum
- d. a cask
- e. a churn

4 What is a man doing if he is pruning?
- a. cutting branches off trees
- b. collecting prunes
- c. cutting hair
- d. collecting plums
- e. cutting flowers

5 All these mean *well known*, but which has an unfavourable meaning?
- a. celebrated
- b. noted
- c. notorious
- d. eminent
- e. famous

6 A man who guards men in prison is

a. a guard
b. a keeper
c. a sentry
d. a warder
e. a porter

7 If you lie or sit awkwardly, you are likely to get . . . and needles in your limbs.

a. tacks
b. pins
c. stitches
d. stabs
e. prickles

8 When a child in the USA is in the first grade at school, a child in Britain is in the

a. first form
b. first set
c. first group
d. first division
e. first class

9 We usually talk about a . . . mistake.

a. neglectful
b. careless
c. negligent
d. heedless
e. reckless

10 All these words mean *a copy*: which one is made to deceive people?

a. a duplicate
b. a replica
c. a model
d. an imitation
e. a counterfeit

11 If someone calls you and your friends a lot of sheep, he means that you
   a. make a lot of noise
   b. are all alike
   c. all have the same kind of hair
   d. follow each other without thinking
   e. don't eat meat

☐

12 Where are coins made?
   a. in a factory
   b. in a workshop
   c. in a laboratory
   d. in a studio
   e. in a mint

☐

13 Which phrase goes with the picture?
   a. a recording angel
   b. off the record
   c. a record player
   d. breaking the record
   e. a public record office

☐

14 Finish this proverb: Two's company, three's
   a. a multitude
   b. a mob
   c. a crowd
   d. a throng
   e. a host

☐

15 Which is correct?
a. Columbus discovered America.
b. Columbus invented America.
c. Columbus identified America.
d. Columbus located America.
e. Columbus detected America.

16 All these words mean *fast*, but which one describes speech?
a. nimble
b. agile
c. rapid
d. express
e. swift

17 This man is
a. prone
b. prostrate
c. level
d. supine
e. even

18 If the police ask a lot of questions of many people, they are carrying out
a. long inquiries
b. outstretched inquiries
c. extensive inquiries
d. elongated inquiries
e. longitudinal inquiries

19 If you refuse to speak to someone you know, you send him to

a. Coventry
b. Manchester
c. Leeds
d. York
e. Bristol

☐

20 Which toy does a small child call *Teddy*?

a. a doll
b. a cat
c. a rabbit
d. a dog
e. a bear

☐

Unit eight

1 The words *seam*, *shaft* and *slag heap* all have something to do with

a. sewing
b. coal mining
c. engineering
d. cars
e. mountains

☐

2 An American says *a parking lot* when an Englishman says

a. a car park
b. a lay-by
c. a garage
d. a car pound
e. parkland

☐

3 Something that is done secretly or slyly is

a. offhand
b. underhand
c. by hand
d. out of hand
e. in hand

4 When you give up all hope of something, you

a. desert hope
b. vacate hope
c. abandon hope
d. throw up hope
e. jettison hope

5 What do you call a ship's record book?

a. a log
b. a diary
c. an autobiography
d. a calendar
e. an album

6 If a baby is born before it is due, it is

a. undue
b. precocious
c. immature
d. previous
e. premature

7 Finish this saying: . . . a day keeps the doctor away.

a. An apple
b. A lemon
c. A pear
d. An orange
e. A banana

8 Which of these goes with the picture?
a. spring to your feet
b. spring a leak
c. a springboard
d. a late spring
e. a hot spring

9 There is a connection between four of these words: which is the odd one?
a. pick
b. poker
c. tongs
d. fireguard
e. shovel

10 If you see red, you
a. have got your eyes closed
b. are angry
c. are unconscious
d. feel sick
e. suffer from high blood pressure

11 A bottleneck is part of a bottle: it can also mean
a. a man who drinks too much
b. a stiff neck

c. the tight neck of a jumper
d. a narrow place where traffic is likely to be congested
e. a sore throat

☐

12 What would you do with a very hot drink?
a. drink it
b. imbibe it
c. sip it
d. quaff it
e. lap it

☐

13 Which of these is shortest?
a. a sword
b. a scimitar
c. a sabre
d. a dagger
e. a cutlass

☐

14 Which does not mean *I'm very confused*?
a. I'm all at sea.
b. I'm completely lost.
c. I'm all at sixes and sevens.
d. I've had one over the eight.
e. I don't know whether I'm coming or going.

☐

15 Which word would you use for the speed of a rocket?
a. celerity
b. quickness
c. agility
d. velocity
e. rapidity

☐

16 Which is correct?
a. a brood of puppies
b. a host of puppies
c. a litter of puppies
d. a tribe of puppies
e. a clutch of puppies

17 Finish this phrase: as steady as
a. a crag
b. a rock
c. a pebble
d. a boulder
e. a stone

18 Which of these goes with the picture?
a. a casting vote
b. downcast
c. casting off
d. cast-offs
e. cast iron

19 A man who is still training to be a soldier is
a. an apprentice
b. a novice
c. a pupil
d. a student
e. a recruit

20 Which of these words would you not use to describe birds singing?
a. warbling
b. trilling
c. chirping
d. chanting
e. whistling

Unit nine

1 Which of these is wrong?
a. a cold frame
b. a picture frame
c. the human frame
d. a frame of mind
e. an up frame

2 Which of these has the idea of permanency?
a. harmed
b. injured
c. wounded
d. maimed
e. hurt

3 Which do we use to serve soup?
a. a spoon
b. a spatula
c. a ladle
d. a scoop
e. a shovel

4 Where did Humpty Dumpty sit?
a. on a tuffet
b. on top of a hill
c. in a corner
d. on the tree top
e. on a wall

5 To stop someone talking, you would
a. shackle him
b. gag him
c. fetter him
d. handcuff him
e. bind him

6 A derelict house has been allowed to go to . . . and ruin.
a. rubble
b. wreck
c. rack
d. neglect
e. rot

7 Which of these means *relatives*?
a. blood sports
b. your own flesh and blood
c. blood donors
d. blood vessels
e. in cold blood

8 An American says *a freeway* when an Englishman says
a. a street
b. a main road
c. a highway
d. a motorway
e. a thoroughfare

9 When a son looks like his father, you can see
a. the image
b. the semblance
c. the resemblance
d. the similitude
e. the copy

10 What do you call the list at the back of a book which tells you where words or subjects may be found in the book?
a. the catalogue
b. the register
c. the index
d. the account
e. the tally

11 All these words mean *talking*. Which means *talking about unimportant things*?
a. conversing
b. conferring
c. discussing
d. nattering
e. interviewing

12 The words *gill*, *fin* and *scales* all have something to do with
a. fish
b. music
c. measures
d. aeroplanes
e. weights

13 Which of these is nearest in meaning to *good-natured*?
a. humane
b. philanthropic
c. charitable
d. amiable
e. benevolent

14 Which of these goes with the picture?
a. snapping his head off
b. a cold snap
c. a snap election
d. a snapshot
e. a snapdragon

15 Which of these is wrong?
a. His voice agitated.
b. His voice quaked.
c. His voice quavered.
d. His voice quivered.
e. His voice trembled.

16 If you suffer from an illness which keeps on returning, it is
a. a recurrent illness
b. a frequent illness
c. a renewed illness
d. a constant illness
e. a habitual illness

17 Which phrase goes with the picture?
a. at close quarters
b. asking for quarter
c. from all quarters
d. the lowest quarters
e. the hind quarters

18 Finish this saying: Out of the . . . into the fire.
a. pot
b. frying pan
c. saucepan
d. cauldron
e. kettle

19 When you promise not to talk about something, you say
a. I won't have a word.
b. I won't whisper a word.
c. I won't announce a word.
d. I won't breathe a word.
e. I won't tell a word.

20 Finish this phrase: as quiet as
a. a mole
b. a beaver
c. a mouse
d. a rat
e. a rodent

Unit ten

1 A bevy is a group of
a. beautiful girls
b. old age pensioners
c. bushes
d. actors
e. loaves of bread

2 A well-known children's rhyme goes: One two, buckle my shoe. Three four,
a. knock at the door
b. fill it with straw
c. let's go to war
d. my foot is sore
e. give me some more

3 Which word describes a plant that is white because it has had no light?
a. blanched
b. bleached
c. snowy
d. milky
e. chalky

4 Which of these is wrong?
a. in the neighbourhood
b. in the vicinity
c. in the surrounding
d. in the district
e. in the locality

5 A notice in a house window saying *B and B* means
a. bed and breakfast
b. bread and butter
c. butcher and baker
d. bring and buy
e. back at bedtime

6 A phrase meaning *unharmed* is
a. safe and secure
b. safe and sure
c. safe and snug
d. safe and sound
e. safe and protected

7 If you know the ropes, you are
a. very experienced at something
b. a sailor
c. a Boy Scout
d. a mountaineer
e. a hangman

8 Which of these words does not mean *brave*?
a. dauntless
b. risky
c. intrepid
d. bold
e. daring

9 A catty remark is
a. a shrewd remark
b. a kindly remark
c. an innocent remark
d. a meaningful remark
e. a spiteful remark

10 If someone tells you that he works in the big top, he works
a. in a flying saucer
b. wearing a large hat
c. in a large attic
d. in a capital city
e. in a circus tent

11 The words *dial, mainspring* and *pendulum* all have something to do with
a. radio
b. telephones
c. seasons of the year
d. clocks
e. watches

12 Finish this phrase: as large as
a. being
b. life
c. being alive
d. existence
e. living

13 Which of these goes with the picture?
a. a forward roll
b. roll call
c. a roll of honour
d. a roll of drums
e. a Swiss roll

14 When your patience is exhausted you might say, *I'm at the end of my . . .*

a. leash
b. lead
c. tether
d. chain
e. mooring

☐

15 Which of these does not necessarily describe someone who is not well?

a. dizzy
b. seedy
c. indisposed
d. ill
e. unwell

☐

16 Which of these is wrong?

a. I'm reluctant to go.
b. I'm unwilling to go.
c. I'm loathe to go.
d. I'm averse to go.
e. I'm disinclined to go.

☐

17 What sound does a turkey make?

a. cooing
b. cackling
c. screeching
d. clucking
e. gobbling

☐

18 An American says *a windshield* when an Englishman says

a. a windcheater
b. a windscreen
c. a windjammer
d. a windfall
e. a wind-break

☐

19 This is a . . . take-off.
   a. upright
   b. erect
   c. upstanding
   d. perpendicular
   e. vertical

☐

20 The chief actress in a play is called
   a. the leading lady
   b. the main lady
   c. the first lady
   d. the foremost lady
   e. the primary lady

☐

Unit eleven

1 If a person has good eyesight, his eyes are
   a. acute
   b. spiked
   c. prickly
   d. barbed
   e. sharp

☐

2 Finish this phrase: the thin end of the . . .
   a. wedge
   b. branch
   c. stick
   d. rod
   e. triangle

☐

3 A wallflower is a garden flower, but it can also mean
- a. a girl at a dance who cannot find a partner
- b. a wall painting
- c. a picture made from pressed flowers
- d. the pattern of cracks in an old wall
- e. a sundial

☐

4 When you are hungry, you feel
- a. vacant
- b. blank
- c. void
- d. unoccupied
- e. empty

☐

5 When you want a letter to arrive quickly, what do you write on it?
- a. Necessary
- b. Imperative
- c. Urgent
- d. Essential
- e. Pressing

☐

6 All these mean *to walk slowly*: which one is used about an injured person?
- a. to ramble
- b. to stroll
- c. to stagger
- d. to saunter
- e. to amble

☐

7 What is this?
- a. a fork-lift
- b. a tuning fork
- c. a fish fork
- d. a trident
- e. a pitchfork

☐

8 Another way of saying *in a straight line* is
a. as the robin flies
b. as the eagle flies
c. as the crow flies
d. as the owl flies
e. as the bird flies

9 Which of these can you not cut?
a. a pack of cards
b. corners
c. hair
d. weight
e. prices

10 Which word would you not use to describe flowers?
a. a bunch
b. a thicket
c. a posy
d. a nosegay
e. a garland

11 Which of these ways of pulling is a sudden movement?
a. hauling
b. jerking
c. heaving
d. dragging
e. towing

12 Who is going to have a baby?
a. an optimistic mother
b. a hopeful mother
c. a confident mother
d. a sanguine mother
e. an expectant mother

13 All these words mean *cold*: which one would you not use to describe the weather?
a. chilly
b. cool
c. bleak
d. icy
e. refrigerated

☐

14 When a person says: *I always call a spade a spade,* it means he is
a. a card player
b. a gardener
c. blunt
d. a grave-digger
e. longwinded

☐

15 Which man does not work in a studio?
a. an artist
b. a broadcaster
c. a designer
d. a photographer
e. a dentist

☐

16 If a friend invites you to see his new issues, he is
a. a stamp collector
b. a proud father
c. a gardener
d. a newspaperman
e. a publisher

☐

17 Which of these means *surprised and sorry*?
a. dismayed
b. frightened
c. horrified
d. terrified
e. petrified

☐

18 Which phrase goes with the picture?
a. jumping the queue
b. jumping down his throat
c. jumping out of his skin
d. jumping at an idea
e. jumping to it

19 An American says *period* when an Englishman says
a. comma
b. hyphen
c. semicolon
d. colon
e. full stop

20 A man with a strong personality is a . . . person.
a. forceful
b. sturdy
c. potent
d. stout
e. mighty

Unit twelve

1 If we call someone an ass, we mean that he
   a. has big ears
   b. is silly
   c. is very docile
   d. is stubborn
   e. has a loud, braying voice

2 Which of these describes a person who was born in London?
   a. a resident of London
   b. an inhabitant of London
   c. a dweller in London
   d. an aboriginal of London
   e. a native of London

3 When you make a very careful and thorough search, you look in every nook and
   a. ingle
   b. corner
   c. chink
   d. cranny
   e. hole

4 Which of these is wrong?
   a. a sensitive shout
   b. sensitive skin
   c. a sensitive plant
   d. a sensitive film
   e. a sensitive artist

5 If your house is near the station, it is . . . for the trains.
a. handy d. adjacent
b. intimate e. nigh
c. neighbouring

6 Replace the word *possible* in this sentence: Is it possible to swim from England to France?
a. probable d. workable
b. feasible e. capable
c. conceivable

7 The abbreviation c/o means
a. Commanding Officer
b. cash with order
c. carry on
d. care of
e. Company

8 Which of these is a funny drawing of a person?
a. a parody d. an imitation
b. a caricature e. an image
c. a counterfeit

9 You can talk about *sending* or *carrying* messages, but which of these would you not say?
a. transporting a message
b. bearing a message
c. conveying a message
d. transmitting a message
e. delivering a message

10 Which phrase goes with the picture?
a. dropping a brick
b. dropping off
c. dropping in
d. dropping a line
e. dropping through

11 An American calls it *a bill*: an Englishman calls it
a. a receipt
b. a check
c. a cheque
d. a banknote
e. an account

12 What would you call a clock that keeps good time?
a. true
b. genuine
c. reliable
d. unerring
e. authentic

13 Finish this proverb: Birds of a feather . . . together.
a. keep
b. meet
c. go
d. flock
e. gather

14 Which noise does a brook make?
a. babbling
b. rustling
c. swishing
d. tinkling
e. pattering

15 When you push someone's head under the water in fun, what are you doing?
a. ducking him
b. submerging him
c. sinking him
d. liquidating him
e. watering him

16 What does it mean if someone is very attached to you?
a. He works closely with you.
b. He likes you very much.
c. You are tied together.
d. He works under you.
e. You like him very much.

17 Which would you not find in a rock?
a. a crack
b. a crevice
c. a slit
d. a fissure
e. a cleft

18 Which phrase goes with the picture?
a. an eightsome reel
b. reeling off a list
c. reeling in
d. reeling from side to side
e. a reel of cotton

19 Which of these is against the law?
a. a fault
b. a vice
c. a sin
d. a crime
e. a defect

20 All these mean *walking slowly and aimlessly*, but which one can also mean *talking aimlessly and at length*?
a. wandering
b. roaming
c. rambling
d. strolling
e. sauntering

Unit thirteen

1 What sort of person would you call a shark?
a. someone with sharp teeth
b. a strong swimmer
c. a murderer
d. someone who is fond of fish
e. a swindler

2 What is the top point of a triangle called?
a. the summit
b. the zenith
c. the crest
d. the climax
e. the apex

3 Which of these is wrong?
a. the next year
b. the succeeding year
c. the subsequent year
d. the following year
e. the consecutive year

☐

4 When someone you know dies, you send the family your
a. pity
b. condolences
c. regret
d. compassion
e. sorrow

☐

5 If you are hard-up, you are
a. harsh
b. quick-tempered
c. tough
d. callous
e. short of money

☐

6 Complete this phrase: hale and
a. snow
b. stout
c. farewell
d. hearty
e. robust

☐

7 Which of these is wrong?
a. iron filings
b. nail filings
c. a filing cabinet
d. in single file
e. a filing clerk

☐

8 When a doctor examines a patient, he is looking for

a. symbols
b. clues
c. hints
d. emblems
e. symptoms

9 All these words mean *amusing*, but which means *amusing and clever*?

a. funny
b. comic
c. droll
d. witty
e. humorous

10 An American says *potato chips* when an Englishman says

a. baked potatoes
b. chips
c. French fried
d. potato croquettes
e. potato crisps

11 Which of these goes with the picture?

a. a pipeline
b. Pipe down!
c. a windpipe
d. bagpipes
e. a blowpipe

12 Someone shows you your signature. What do you say if you recognise it?
a. Yes, it's faultless.
b. Yes, it's reliable.
c. Yes, it's true.
d. Yes, it's correct.
e. Yes, it's genuine.

13 The words *pane*, *sash cord* and *sill* all have something to do with
a. doctors
b. glassmaking
c. hospitals
d. doors
e. windows

14 British doctors do not have a trade union, they have a professional
a. society
b. club
c. association
d. league
e. syndicate

15 If a boat leans over to one side, it has got
a. a slope
b. a list
c. a slant
d. a gradient
e. an incline

16 Which of these describes a person's height?
a. stature
b. altitude
c. highness
d. elevation
e. eminence

17 Finish this proverb: Honesty is the best
a. scheme
b. plan
c. strategy
d. practice
e. policy

18 If someone tells you something tongue-in-cheek, you
a. feel sorry for him
b. would be offended
c. know it's a secret
d. don't take him seriously
e. agree with him

19 What is this?
a. a bay window
b. a bow window
c. a French window
d. a casement
e. a dormer window

20 When a river turns many corners, we say it
a. contorts
b. coils
c. undulates
d. twists
e. meanders

Unit fourteen

1 What is a chatterbox?
a. a gossip column in a newspaper
b. a slang word for a radio
c. a refrigerator
d. a talkative person
e. a telephone kiosk

2 All these are colours, but which is also the name of a precious stone?
a. fawn
b. turquoise
c. indigo
d. mauve
e. purple

3 In which four ways do British people usually cook eggs?
a. boil bake stew fry
b. poach boil stew fry
c. fry boil scramble poach
d. scramble steam broil grill
e. grill fry simmer stew

4 What does a spanner do to a nut?
a. it unties it
b. it liberates it
c. it slackens it
d. it unlooses it
e. it releases it

5 Which of these would you never hear on a radio news programme?
a. Here is the latest information.
b. Here are some new tidings.
c. Here is a recent report.
d. Here is the late bulletin.
e. Here is a news flash.

☐

6 An American talks about *an icebox* when an Englishman says
a. a cold store
b. a deep freeze
c. a freezer
d. a cooler
e. a fridge

☐

7 All these are man-made channels for water: which is usually the widest?
a. a drain
b. a ditch
c. a canal
d. a gutter
e. a gully

☐

8 Finish this sentence: Don't beat about the
a. tree
b. shrub
c. bush
d. bracken
e. undergrowth

☐

9 Which of these is nearest in meaning to *absurd*?
a. ridiculous
b. hilarious
c. comic
d. amusing
e. humorous

☐

10 Which of these is different in meaning from the others?
a. a loyal friend
b. a true friend
c. a faithful friend
d. a devoted friend
e. a law-abiding friend

☐

11 Which of these crowds is most likely to be angry or excited?
a. The crowd met in the street.
b. The crowd gathered in the street.
c. The crowd swarmed into the street.
d. The crowd congregated in the street.
e. The crowd collected in the street.

☐

12 When you enter for a race, you are
a. a candidate
b. a competitor
c. an applicant
d. a claimant
e. an opponent

☐

13 An American says *a sidewalk* when an Englishman says
a. a pavement
b. a track
c. a footpath
d. a gangway
e. a walkway

☐

14 The words *extraction, filling* and *drilling* all have something to do with
a. roads
b. medicine
c. oil wells
d. dentists
e. woodwork

☐

15 Which phrase goes with the picture?
a. playing truant
b. playing the fool
c. playing the game
d. playing second fiddle
e. playing to the gallery

16 What's the difference between a cape and a cloak?
a. They are both the same.
b. A cape is shorter than a cloak.
c. They are different but they are both short.
d. They are different but they are both long.
e. A cloak is shorter than a cape.

17 Which of these is wrong?
a. prime minister
b. prime beef
c. prime education
d. prime numbers
e. prime cost

18 All these are round, but which is also flat?

a. a bulb
b. a globe
c. a sphere
d. a disc
e. an orb

19 Which of these goes with the picture?

a. a point of honour
b. point-blank range
c. a turning point
d. Come to the point!
e. a point of view

20 Complete this phrase: as blind as

a. a mole
b. a bat
c. a toad
d. a ferret
e. a fox

Unit fifteen

1 Dukes, lords and princes are members of the
a. upper classes
b. upper ranks
c. first grades
d. higher degrees
e. primary stages

2 Finish this phrase: as sober as
a. a juror
b. a barrister
c. a solicitor
d. a lawyer
e. a judge

3 When a wheel has turned round once completely, it has made
a. a revolution
b. a twist
c. a circulation
d. a rotation
e. a turn

4 In England you might see the sign *Free House*
a. outside a public house
b. in an estate agent's window
c. outside the Houses of Parliament
d. on a house for sale
e. outside a church

5 When someone is obsessed by an idea, he has a bee in his
a. cap
b. bonnet
c. hat
d. hair
e. wig

6 Which of these means *He fell down*?
a. He measured his length.
b. He measured his range.
c. He measured his spread.
d. He measured his stretch.
e. He measured his extent.

7 Electricity is a form of
a. energy
b. strength
c. potential
d. vigour
e. force

8 The words *setting*, *cutting* and *polishing* all have something to do with
a. the sun
b. railways
c. floors
d. glassmaking
e. jewels

9 Which of these goes with the picture?
a. a running track
b. twin track
c. a one-track mind
d. track it down
e. cover up your tracks

10 If someone always arrives on time, you would call him
a. accurate
b. precise
c. exact
d. punctual
e. correct

11 If you lead someone up the garden path,
a. you are showing him your prize flowers
b. you are misleading him
c. you are saying goodbye
d. you are a gardener
e. he has just arrived at your house

12 Which of these colours does not describe a person's hair?
a. yellow
b. tawny
c. golden
d. sandy
e. buff

13 These are all ways of laughing, but which can also show anger?
a. tittering
b. cackling
c. giggling
d. bellowing
e. chuckling

14 Which of these is never thrown by hand?
a. a harpoon
b. a javelin
c. an arrow
d. a spear
e. a dart

15 A small, round, brown mark on the skin is called
a. a spot
b. a speck
c. a flaw
d. a smudge
e. a mole

16 What would be most likely to make a swishing sound?
a. a log fire
b. meat roasting in the oven
c. long silk curtains
d. a loose floorboard
e. a vacuum cleaner

17 Which is usually dirty?
a. froth
b. spray
c. scum
d. spume
e. lather

18 When something has been made quickly and not very carefully, it is rough and
a. ready
b. tumble
c. smooth
d. rocky
e. tough

19 This bath is
a. overflowing
b. flowing
c. leaking
d. dripping
e. dribbling

20 All these are stories, but which is the shortest?
a. a tale
b. an anecdote
c. a narrative
d. an account
e. a legend

Answers

Unit one

1 **c.** *Insolent* = deliberately very rude.
2 **a.** All these support clothing. *Garters* and *suspenders* = supports for stockings. *Braces* (US suspenders) and *belts* = supports for trousers. *Girdles* = belts of various kinds, usually worn by women, often to improve the figure (a roll-on).
3 **b.** Also, *a turntable* = a rotating platform to turn trains round. Notice: a turncoat = *a traitor*. Table legs can be made on a lathe, a machine used in wood-turning.
4 **c.** All these words = not strong. We talk of *frail*, *weak* or *sickly* people. We say: There's a *faint* chance, a *faint* possibility; but usually: His chances are *slim*.
5 **d.** *A veritable Picasso* = an artist, who is as good as Picasso. All the others = a painting which is actually by Picasso.
6 **c.** All these give support, but the aid to walking in the picture is *a crutch*. *A prop* = a wooden post to hold up a line of clothes hung out to dry (a clothes prop); also, a support for the roof of a mine (a pit prop). *A stand* = a support or holder (a cake stand, a hat stand, an umbrella stand).
7 **c.** *As fit as a fiddle* = (a fixed phrase) in excellent health. All five words = musical instruments with strings.
8 **d.** Of these five words, only *an accomplice* always has a bad sense. *A collaborator* works with someone, sometimes in a bad sense (to collaborate with the enemy). *A partner* works with someone (a business partner), or plays with someone (a tennis partner, a bridge partner, a dancing

partner). *An aide* = an assistant to an important political or military person. *An ally* supports or helps, often in a war or an argument.

9 **c.** All the others are correct. We say: *The chauffeur started the engine. He didn't stir a muscle* = He didn't move at all.

10 **d.** All the others are wrong. We *submit* a suggestion, *propound* a thesis, *propose* or *suggest* a plan.

11 **b.** We talk about the courses of a meal. All the others are correct. *A branch* = an offshoot, or a smaller part which divides off (the French branch of the family).

12 **c.** A ship is left *high and dry* on the shore when the tide goes out. So, high and dry = (metaphorically) left without money or help. Notice: I'm dry = I'm thirsty.

13 **a.** *One man's meat is another man's poison* = things that are good for one person are bad for others. All five words = food. *Victuals* is an old-fashioned word. *Grub* is slang. *Fodder* = food for cattle and horses, never for humans.

14 **e.** *Lanky* = tall, thin and awkward. *Elevated, exalted* and *lofty* men are usually dignified and important. Notice: Lofty is sometimes a slang name for a tall man. He's *high* = (colloquial) he is drunk or drugged.

15 **b.** (A fixed phrase.) A *hit or miss* attempt = an attempt which may or may not succeed. We never use the other answers.

16 **b.** A large shop (a department store) might have a furniture *department*, an electrical *department*, etc. All five words are sub-groups of larger units: *classes* of words, children, hotels, etc; *categories* of hotels, books, etc; *divisions* of soldiers, workers, football teams; *sections* of land, workers, soldiers. A section is usually smaller than a division: a small building firm

would have a paint section; a large chemical company would have a paint division.

17 **d.** All five words = books giving information, but only *an atlas* has maps. We have telephone and business *directories*; railway and school *timetables*. *A biography* = the true story of a person's life.

18 **d.** *To set out* = to start a journey. *To set the pace* = to lead others, as in a race, by deciding the speed; also, to set a standard of behaviour, etc. *To set sail* = to start a voyage (of ships). *To set your house in order* = to put your affairs straight. *To set the fashion* = to lead others in dress, behaviour.

19 **b.** *A vice* = a wooden or metal tool for gripping things. *A plane* = a tool for smoothing wood; also, an aeroplane. *A mallet* = a wooden hammer.

20 **b.** *To look vacant* = to have a blank expression on your face. Notice: to save face = to avoid humiliation.

Unit two

1 **a.** This is a favourite nursery rhyme which continues:

Yes sir, yes sir, three bags full.

2 **c.** *Polite* and *courteous* = well-mannered, though courteous is the more formal. *Gallant* (here) describes a man who is very attentive to ladies. *Cultivated, refined* and *polished* refer to more than politeness, being used of highly cultured people, suggesting good taste.

3 **b.** All five words are metals, but we only say *as bold as brass*. Notice: brazen = (literally) made of brass. We talk of a brazen voice or woman, meaning they are loud, vulgar.

4 **a.** The idiom goes back to the British Admiral, Lord Nelson, who ignored the order to retreat by putting his telescope to his blind eye when looking at the signal. *A blind corner* = a corner you cannot easily see round (especially when driving).

5 **d.** *To paddle* = to walk bare-footed in shallow water, e.g. at the edge of the sea; also, to drive a canoe along with a paddle (the same as *to canoe*). *To row* = to use two oars to move a boat from a sitting position. *To scull* = to move a boat using one oar twisted from side to side at the stern from a standing position. *To sail* = to ride in a boat which has sails.

6 **b.** You *book in* at a hotel, when you sign the book. You are *booked up* when you have no spare time. You *book* seats (at the theatre, or for a concert) by ordering them in advance. When you are *booked*, you may be a performer engaged for a particular performance, or you may have your name taken and written down by a football referee or a policeman for an offence.

7 **b.** All five words = the highest point: the *crest* of a hill or a wave; the *summit* of a mountain; the *peak* of a mountain; the *apex* of a triangle or a roof.

8 **a.** All five words = to agree, to go well together, but colours only *match*. Clothes or jobs may *suit* you. Things *accord* with your ideas if they are agreeable. Your job should *correspond* with your ambitions and abilities. If two people describe the same thing, their descriptions should *tally*.

9 **a.** *An apartment* = (in Britain) lodgings; rooms taken for a short time. *A villa* = a large house usually outside the town (a holiday villa). *A mansion* = a large, grand house in the city or

in the country. *A bungalow* = a one-storeyed house.

10 **b.** *Surfing* is a sea sport. The surfer swims out to sea, stands on his surf-board and rides to the beach on large in-coming waves. *Fox-hunting* is a blood-sport in which the fox is chased across country by hunters on horseback. *Point-to-point* and *steeplechasing* are cross-country races on horseback. *Show-jumping* is a riding competition, held both in the open and indoors.

11 **a.** *A score* = (here) printed music; also, a grudge (*settling old scores*); also, the number of goals or points in a game (the *half-time score* = the number of goals scored half-way through a game); also, twenty (so here, *scores of times* = many); also, an account (*on more than one score* = on more than one account, for more than one reason).

12 **a.** All five are used at the meal table. *A cruet* = a stand which holds pepper, salt, mustard and vinegar. *A decanter* = a large glass bottle to hold wine. *A punch bowl* = a large bowl for making and serving punch (spiced wine). *A tureen* = a large dish for holding soup.

13 **e.** *Facts and figures* = (a fixed phrase) information or details.

14 **c.** *A forecast* is made with some certainty, on the basis of existing information. We forecast the weather, sales, expenses, or even football results. *A prophecy* (literally) tells of the future, but is made by a prophet, who claims to know the will of God. *A premonition* = a feeling or warning that something, usually bad, is going to happen. *A prediction* tells of the future, using the stars, playing cards or other unscientific methods. *Anticipation* = looking forward into the future, usually to something pleasant.

15 **a.** *Numb* and *insensitive* = without feeling. You can become numb with cold, after an injection, from a shock, or sometimes if you sit awkwardly for a long time your foot or leg can go numb. *Painless* = without pain and (metaphorically) without difficulties (a painless experience). *Senseless* = stupid, the opposite of sensible; also, unconscious, having lost your senses. *Unfeeling* = cold (of a person), unemotional. *Nonsensical* = not making sense (nonsensical remarks).

16 **c.** *A gangway* = a narrow walkway with a handrail (a gang-plank has no handrail). *A pontoon* = a floating support for a bridge. *A drawbridge* = a bridge that can be raised or lowered, as at the entrance to a castle. *A catwalk* = a narrow footway, often high up, (in a ship's engine room).

17 **e.** All these words = to get smaller. Clothes sometimes *shrink* when they are washed. Things *shrivel* with age (leaves and old people's skin, becoming curled and wrinkled). Money or food *diminishes* when there is less of it. Metal *contracts* when it is cold (expands when hot).

18 **e.** *To break down* = to burst into tears. *To break the ice* = (metaphorically) to overcome shyness or formality. *To break the news* = to announce (usually bad) news. *To break out* = to begin (a fire broke out, war broke out), but if a person breaks out, he escapes. *To break your word* (the opposite of to keep your word) = to fail to keep a promise. Notice: a nervous breakdown = a mental collapse.

19 **c.** The correct phrase is *in haste* (He wrote the letter in haste). *In a hurry, in a rush* and *in a scramble* all mean the same (I'm in a hurry, etc). *In a flap* = (colloquial) in a panic, or in a nervous state.

20 **a.** *To falter* = to walk or speak uncertainly. You *limp* if you have a bad foot or a bad leg. You *hobble* when you walk awkwardly, possibly because your feet hurt. Very old or drunken people *totter*, walking unsteadily. *To stagger* is even more unsteady; we stagger when we are hit or pushed and are about to fall.

Unit three

1 **c.** All the others are wrong. Notice: adjectives starting with 'p' often have opposites starting 'im': impossible, imperfect, impolite, etc.

2 **e.** *A span* = a length of time or distance (from one end of *a bridge* to the other, from the thumb to the outstretched little finger); we say: The bridge spanned the river. A *suspension* bridge = a bridge with towers at both ends, joined by a wire cable: the bridge itself is suspended from this. *A cantilever* = a supporting bracket (as used in some bridges).

3 **e.** *A career* = (often) a lifetime's work. *A job* = (informal) *an appointment, position* or *post*. Jobs usually have less responsibility than appointments, etc, but most people refer, informally, to their job.

4 **e.** (A fixed phrase.) *A fable* = a short animal story with a moral. *A parable* = a short, simple story with a hidden moral meaning, as in the Bible. *An anecdote* = a short, incidental story.

5 **a.** *A flue* = a narrow chimney or ventilating pipe. *A channel* = a passage along which water flows. *A main* = the biggest pipe that carries gas or water into a house. *An artery* = a pipe that carries blood round the body. *A hose* = a rubber or plastic water pipe (we water the garden with a hose).

6 **e.** A well-known nursery rhyme goes:

> Little Bo-beep, she lost her sheep
> And didn't know where to find them.
> Leave them alone, and they'll come home,
> Bringing their tails behind them.

7 **e.** *As cool as a cucumber* = (a fixed phrase) very calm, not excited.

8 **e.** All these are used for different trades and operations. We talk of medical, electrical, kitchen and fire-fighting *appliances*; surgical, scientific, measuring and musical *instruments*; military, gardening, farming and household *equipment*; sailing and fishing *tackle*; chemical, breathing, gymnastic and heating *apparatus*.

9 **a.** A milkman's daily calls = his *round*. Postmen, newspaper delivery boys, doctors in hospitals also have a daily round. *A round of toast* = a slice of toast. *A round number* = a number ending in nought (10, 200, 3000, etc); also, an approximate number (a price of £201 could be called £200 in round numbers). Notice: a round dozen = a full dozen. *A round of drinks* = a drink for everyone in a group. *A roundabout* = a traffic island.

10 **d.** *Man to man* (a fixed phrase) is always used of people talking.

11 **a.** These are all table games.

12 **e.** At the *outset* = at the *beginning*, at first. *An origin* = a starting point, a cause (the origin of an argument, a man of humble origins). *An introduction* = opening remarks; information leading up to the main subject (an introduction to a radio programme, a book, a lecture).

13 **d**

14 **a.** *A quest* = (formal, literary) *a search* (in quest of a wife, in the quest for a wife). *An inquest* = an official investigation to find out the cause of an unexplained death.

15 **d.** All birds have *a bill,* or beak, but we never talk of a bill bird. *A bill of fare* = a menu. *A bill of sale* = a notice advertising a sale; also, a receipt. *A bill sticker* = a man who sticks up bills, or posters. Your doctor gives you *a clean bill of health* when he says you are fit.

16 **e.** We would never talk about a *dear* jewel, but we would use all the other words. *Priceless* = beyond having a price. *Costly* and *expensive* = of a very high price. *Precious* = worth a great deal, valuable, but it expresses no idea of price.

17 **a.** *A tip-off* = the secret giving of information, or a signal, often betraying someone to the police. When something is *on the tip of your tongue,* you are just about to say it. *Leaving a tip* = leaving a small amount of money for a service (for a hairdresser or a waiter). *On tip-toe* = standing or walking on the tips of your toes, either to be taller or to be quiet. *A rubbish tip* = a place where rubbish is thrown away in a large heap.

18 **d.** The proverb means that it is better to have one thing certain than the possibility of two.

19 **c.** *Unpalatable* = unpleasant to taste (food or drink). The other four refer to people or things you cannot tolerate.

20 **a.** *Flimsy* = weak, easily destroyed (flimsy paper, flimsy material, flimsy excuses). All the others = very small or unimportant differences.

Unit four

1 **b.** The rhyme continues:

Four and twenty blackbirds, baked in a pie.

Notice: in Britain, *wheat, oats, barley* and *rye* are all called *corn,* though corn most commonly refers to wheat. They are all cereals.

2 **b.** We also talk about the *hub* of interest, or the hub of activity. We talk of the *heart* of a cabbage, the country, a forest; the *nucleus* of an atom, an idea, a crowd; the *core* of an apple, or a subject; the *focus* of a lens, of attention, of trouble.

3 **a.** *Rose* and *pink* = very pale red. *Scarlet* = bright red. *Crimson* = dark red, the colour of blood. *Maroon* = brownish-red.

4 **e.** This is baby-talk. Notice: Bye-bye = Goodbye.

5 **e.** (A fixed phrase.) We talk of a *hand-to-mouth* existence. The other phrases have no meaning.

6 **d.** *As easy as winking* = (a fixed phrase) very easy. We also say: As easy as falling off a log. *Forty winks* = a short sleep, usually not in bed. *Dropping off* = falling asleep.

7 **b.** *A talk* = a friendly *conversation* (to have a talk) or a lecture (to give a talk on stamp-collecting). *A chat* = an informal conversation (to have a chat). *An interview* = a formal meeting where one person asks another person questions, to find out information (an interview for a job, an interview with the police). *A discussion* = an informal debate, where two or more people talk about one topic.

8 **d.** The hammer in a bell that strikes it = a clapper. *A bell push* = the button of an electric bell. *A bell ringer* = a person who rings bells (church bells). *A bell tent* = a tent shaped like a bell, being round and pointed. *A bell tower* = a tower, usually in a church, that holds the bells.

9 **d**

10 **e.** *A pack of cards* = the fifty-two playing cards, one on top of the other. They are never called *a set of cards*. *A hand of cards* = those cards you hold in your hand, which the dealer deals

to you. (Don't show your hand.) *A stack* = a high heap of something (a haystack). *A packet* = a container, but even if the cards are in their packet, we would still call them a pack (to open a new pack of cards).

11 **b.** The proverb means, having been hurt, we are timid of a thing on a later occasion.

12 **a.** *Weatherbeaten* = made rough and brown by the weather.

13 **a.** Notice: *soaked through* = very wet.

14 **a.** *To show off* = to try to impress people, often because you think you are clever. *To demonstrate* = (formal) *to show* (a car salesman demonstrates a new car). *To exhibit* = to show to the public (an artist exhibits his paintings). *To display* = to arrange things to be admired or bought (a model displays new dresses).

15 **a.** The *late* king = the former, or dead king. The late champion = the previous champion.

16 **e.** *A theatre play* ends. *Sugar* and *salt* change into a liquid when put in water. When *a marriage* is *dissolved*, it is ended. When *Parliament* dissolves, there is an election to vote for a new Parliament.

17 **a.** All the words = *to throw*, though *to toss* and *to fling* are quite strong. We *launch* ships, gliders, a business, an attack, or an arrow.

18 **c.** People and physical things can be *weak*. *Shaky* = unsteady (a shaky table, shaky writing, a shaky voice). *Limp* = not stiff (limp paper; cats go limp when picked up). *Frail* = easily damaged (a frail glass ornament, a frail old lady).

19 **d.** *A set-to* = a short fight. *The jet set* = fashionable, young rich people who use jet planes. *A set square* = a wooden triangular shape for drawing angles. *On set* = on a film set, acting. *A portable set* = a radio or television set which can be carried about.

20 **d.** You have *altered* = you are different (in appearance, character). The other three are wrong.

Unit five

1 **e.** *An occupier* = a person who is in occupation, whether a tenant or an owner. We talk about *residents* of a street or block of flats. *Population* = all who live in a town, city or country. We talk about the *inhabitants* of a house, street or town. *A dweller* is mostly used in town-dweller, cave-dweller, etc.

2 **e.** *He spread out his hand* = he opened the fingers of his hand. All the others = he moved his hand forward (perhaps to shake hands or take hold of something).

3 **c.** *As flat as a pancake* = (a fixed phrase) completely flat. Notice: *wafer*-thin (an advertisement might claim that a wrist watch is wafer-thin).

4 **a.** *Infinite* = without limits (infinite wisdom, mercy). All the other words = going on for a long time; never-ending.

5 **e.** *A caretaker* might perform the duties of all of the others.

6 **e.** All the others = different ways of punishing by putting to death.

7 **d.** *A plinth* = a square block on which a pillar or statue stands.

8 **b.** *To take a dim view* = (an idiom) to disapprove. You have a dim view (literally) if you cannot see something clearly.

9 **d.** (The phrase has no meaning.) *An identity card* = an official card to show who you are. *An identity disc* = a tag worn round the neck or wrist to show who you are (dogs often have one on their collars). Police sometimes use *an*

identity parade for witnesses to pick out one person from a group. A case of *mistaken identity* is where someone is mistaken for someone else.

10 **d.** The proverb means that all apparently bad things have some good in them.

11 **b.** *An entertainment* = a performance, often at a cinema or theatre. *A festival* = a day or period of celebration (e.g. Christmas). *A festivity* = any special merry occasion. *A reception* = a formal party (a wedding reception).

12 **c.** We *obstruct* a road or the view. *An obstacle* = (literally) an object standing in your way (a big stone on a path); also (metaphorically), a difficult person (an obstacle to progress). *A hindrance* makes things difficult (heavy clothes are a hindrance to a runner). *An impediment* delays or makes difficulties (a speech impediment). *An inhibition* restrains you from action (fat people may be inhibited from wearing swimming costumes).

13 **c.** *Dusk* = the evening half-light (opposite of dawn). *Gloom* and *dimness* = semi-darkness (in a forest, or a windowless room). *Obscurity* and *darkness* = opposite of light. Notice: gloomy = (metaphorically) despondent.

14 **d.** *To answer a charge* = to answer an accusation. The others = I'll pay. *To pay the bill = to settle the account. To defray the expenses* (formal) and *to cover the cost* = to pay a larger amount, possibly several bills (e.g. of a holiday).

15 **e.** *To dissect* = to cut up in order to examine (plants, animals). You *divorce* your husband or wife when you legally end your marriage. *To share out* = to distribute equally. *To divide* = to separate (time, money). *To split* = to break into parts, often with force (to split wood).

16 **c.** *Ecstasy* = a very strong feeling of happiness.

Pleasure and *delight* = enjoyment. We take pleasure or delight in something. *Happiness* = *joy* (to wish someone happiness or joy).

17 **c.** We might call this *a mop* of hair.

18 **e.** *A mouthwash* = a liquid to wash out the mouth. *Dribble* = saliva running from the mouth. *Sweat* and *perspiration* = the moisture that appears on the skin when we are hot or afraid.

19 **b.** *By the skin of your teeth* = (an idiom) only just (escape, succeed). *Armed to the teeth* = very heavily armed. People who have *a sweet tooth* like sweet things to eat. *Fighting tooth and nail* = fighting fiercely, like animals. *Long in the tooth* = old.

20 **a.** *To blow up a tyre* = to put air in it. *A storm blew up* = a storm began. *He blew up* = he suddenly got angry, exploded. *The house blew up* = the house exploded.

Unit six

1 **e.** *Spitting* = occasional spots of rain. *Drizzling* = raining lightly. *Pouring* = raining heavily.

2 **a.** (A fixed phrase.) Notice: *a portion* of cake, *a crumb* of bread.

3 **d.** *A tunnel* = an underground passage. *A burrow* = a hole dug by rabbits and foxes, which has horizontal length and a roof, like a tunnel. *Hollows* and *pits* are open to the sky. *A cavern* = a large cave (caves rarely extend far horizontally). *Excavation* = the digging done by engineers and archaeologists.

4 **d.** *To encounter* = (formal) to meet, usually by chance. *To join* = to go to. *To coincide with* = to agree with; also, to happen to be present at the same time. *To touch* = (slang) to borrow money

from. *To contact* = to get in touch with, meet, telephone, speak to.

5 **c.** *To come across* = to discover. *To come up to* = to approach. *To come for* = to come to get, possibly to buy. *To come by* = to come by way of, calling at; also, to obtain by chance.

6 **d.** (A fixed phrase.) *Buttercups* and *daisies* are wild flowers, the others are garden flowers.

7 **c.** *A drought* = a long period when no rain falls, causing a shortage of water. *A famine* = a severe food shortage. *A dearth* = a shortage (of food, ideas). *A deficiency* = a lack or shortage (of food, causing malnutrition; of money, suggesting possible theft). *A scarcity* = a shortage, less than is demanded (of anything).

8 **b.** All are the results of thinking. To make *a decision* = to make up your mind, to come to *a conclusion*. You show *judgement* if you make good decisions; a judge passes *judgement* on law-breakers after *a verdict* of guilty. Tax inspectors and valuers make *assessments*, decisions about values or amounts of money.

9 **d.** *To be caught red-handed* = to be caught in the act of committing a crime. *Red tape* = official meaningless time-wasting. *To roll out the red carpet* = to give a splendid reception. *A red rag to a bull* = something which makes someone very angry. *A red herring* = something that draws attention away from the important facts. (A smoked – red – herring is used to train dogs to follow a scent.)

10 **c.** *To grip* = to take a tight hold. *To clutch* and *to grasp* = to take a tight hold quickly (in fear or greed). *To clinch* = to hold with the arms as boxers sometimes do.

11 **b.** *Retarded* = held back (retarded progress = slowed-up progress; a retarded child = a mentally slow child). *Tardy* = (formal,

literary) late; slow-moving. *Belated* = coming late (belated arrivals, belated presents, belated travellers). *Overdue* = failing to arrive on time (babies, payments, ships, causing worry).

12 **d.** The proverb means that if you need something badly enough, you will invent an answer to your problem. *A lack* = a shortage (of water, effort, knowledge). *A want* = an absence (of care, money). Notice: to be in want = to be very poor. *A defect* = something wrong or missing (a defect in wood, in an argument; a physical defect). *A necessity* and *a need* = something needed.

13 **e.** We talk about the *chief* of a tribe; the *head* of a school, a business, a family; the *king* of a country; the *master* of a household, a ship (the captain).

14 **d.** British *chemist's shops* sell medicines and cosmetics. *Drugstores* in the USA sell many other things, including ice-cream and soft drinks.

15 **b.** *The handle of a sword* = the hilt. The others are all meanings of *butt*.

16 **e.** *To let your hair down* = to act without restraint or control. *To let someone off* = to forgive him. *To let the cat out of the bag* = to give away a secret. *To let someone down* = to fail to help him. *To let sleeping dogs lie* = to leave alone, not look for trouble.

17 **a.** *A valley* and *a vale* (literary) = the low land between hills. *A trench* = a narrow ditch dug by a spade. *A trough* = the low part of water between waves.

18 **b.** *To clench* = to hold tightly together, usually teeth or fists. We *screw up* our eyes in bright light. We *curl* our toes in fear. We *purse* our lips in disapproval.

19 **a.** *Wretched* = very miserable. *Woebegone*

=showing trouble (a woebegone expression; a woebegone appearance).

20 **c.** (A fixed phrase.) All the others make sense, but we do not use them.

Unit seven

1 **c.** (This is usually found at the bottom of a sheet of paper.) *Pay to order* is sometimes printed on cheques, but is never abbreviated.

2 **c.** *As sound as a bell* = (a fixed phrase) in very good condition, in good health. The other words have no meaning in this phrase.

3 **b.** *A bin* can be box-like (a coal bin, a bread bin) or round (a flour bin, a dustbin) and rubbish bins have many shapes. *A drum* = a metal *barrel*. *A cask* = a small barrel. *A churn* can be for holding large amounts of milk, or for making butter.

4 **a.** *To prune* = to cut off unwanted parts (of trees, plants). *A prune* = a dried plum.

5 **c.** We talk about a *notorious* criminal, thief, liar; a *celebrated* pianist, writer, style; a *noted* politician, building, beauty spot; an *eminent* lawyer, wit, speech.

6 **d.** *A guard* = a soldier (a palace guard); also, an official person (a guard on the railways).
A keeper = a man who looks after zoo animals or a park. *A sentry* = a soldier standing on guard. *A porter* = a door-keeper or a man who carries loads.

7 **b.** (A fixed phrase.)

8 **a.** In British schools, *sets*, *groups* and *divisions* are parts of *a class* or *form*. A form is more often used in secondary schools.

9 **b.** All these are used to describe people, showing varying degrees of carelessness. *Reckless* is the strongest word.

10 **e.** People make *counterfeit* coins, banknotes, documents, etc. *A duplicate* = an exact copy, made with no bad intention (a duplicate key, a duplicate birth-certificate). *A replica* = an exact copy (of a painting, a ship, a building). *A model* = a copy, though usually much smaller than the original. *An imitation* = an attempted copy, usually inferior in some way (imitation jewels, leather). Imitations can be used to deceive people, but only counterfeits are made for that purpose.

11 **d.** The suggestion is that you are weak, without minds of your own.

12 **e.** All these are places of work. British coins are made at the Royal Mint.

13 **d.** *A record* = (here) the existing best performance. *A recording angel* = the mythical being who writes down all men's actions. *Off the record* = unofficially, not written down. *A record player* = an electric gramophone. *The public record office* = the building where all important national documents are kept.

14 **c.** All these words = a large number of people, but the proverb only uses *a crowd*. It means that a third person is usually in the way of the other two.

15 **a.** *To discover* = to find something which has always existed. *To invent* = to make or devise something which did not exist before. *To identify* = to recognise, give a name to something. *To locate* = to find the position of something. *To detect* = to find out, usually by careful examination, like a detective.

16 **c.** *Nimble* and *agile* = fast, neat, when describing movements of the body (nimble fingers, as agile as a monkey). *Express* = fast, but when carrying things (express delivery, mail, trains). *Swift* = fast moving (a swift blow, runner, reply; but rarely a swift car, train).

17 **d.** *Prone* and *prostrate* = lying face downwards, the opposite of *supine*. The others could not be used here.
18 **c.** The others are unlikely. *Outstretched* = extended (an outstretched hand, arm). *Elongated* = made longer. *Longitudinal* = running lengthways (the lines of longitude on a map).
19 **a.** (An idiom.)
20 **e.** *Teddy* is the name for a traditional furry yellow toy bear, named after the American President, Theodore Roosevelt.

Unit eight

1 **b.** *A seam* = the joining of two pieces of cloth; also, a layer of coal underground. *A shaft* = a metal bar (a propellor shaft); also, the vertical opening to a mine. *A slag heap* = the mountain of waste material from a coal mine.
2 **a.** *A lay-by* = a space at the side of a main road for cars to park for a short time without obstructing the traffic. *A car pound* = a place where the police put cars they have taken away for being wrongly parked. *Parkland* = private extensive open land with grass and trees.
3 **b.** *Offhand* = casual, careless (behaviour). *By hand* = manually, not by machine. *Out of hand* = out of control. *In hand* = under control; also, in reserve.
4 **c.** *To desert* = to go away from (your job, your wife). *To vacate* = to leave empty (a house, a post). *To throw up* = to give up (an idea, a job). *To jettison* = to throw things out of a boat or plane to make it lighter.
5 **a.** Also, a log-book.
6 **e.** *Undue* = unwarranted, excessive (expense). *Precocious* = having abilities in advance of your age (a precocious child). *Immature* = not fully

developed (immature ideas, men). *Previous* = earlier (on a previous occasion, a previous speaker).

7 **a.** The saying suggests that the regular eating of apples is healthy.

8 **c.** *To spring to your feet* = to jump up. *To spring a leak* = to weaken so that water comes in (of ships, roofs). *A late spring* = the late arrival of spring weather. *A hot spring* = a stream of hot water coming out of the earth.

9 **a.** *A pick* = a pickaxe, a heavy, double-pointed tool which breaks up the ground. The other four are concerned with domestic fires. *A fireguard* = a protection. *A poker, tongs* and *a shovel* = fire-irons. A pick and shovel are regularly used together.

10 **b.** (An idiom.)

11 **d**

12 **c.** *To sip* = to drink carefully, taking only a small amount each time. *To imbibe* = to drink, but often (metaphorically) to imbibe knowledge. *To quaff* = to drink a large amount at one gulp (to quaff a glass of beer). *To lap* = to drink with the tongue (cats lap milk).

13 **d.** *A dagger* = a knife for fighting. *A scimitar* = a short, curved sword, associated with Islamic countries. *A sabre* = a curved sword used by cavalry. *A cutlass* = a short sword with one cutting edge which was used by sailors.

14 **d.** *To have one over the eight* = (colloquial) to be drunk (having drunk more than eight pints).

15 **d.** *Velocity* is the only one which is measured. *Celerity* = (old-fashioned) quickness (to do things with celerity). *Agility* = physical speed and skill (to run, jump with agility). *Rapidity* = *quickness* (the rapidity of a computer).

16 **c.** We talk about *a brood* of chickens; *a host* of people; *a tribe* of people or relations; *a clutch* of eggs.

17 **b.** (A fixed phrase.) *A crag* = a high, rough rock. *A pebble* = a smooth, small stone (pebbles on the beach). *A boulder* = a large, rounded rock.

18 **c.** *To cast off* = to free a boat from its moorings. *A casting vote* = a deciding vote made by the chairman at a meeting when the other votes are equal. *Downcast* = sad. *Cast-offs* = (colloquial) old, unwanted clothing. *Cast iron* = iron shaped in a mould when melted.

19 **e.** All these are learners. *An apprentice* = a person learning a trade. *A novice* = a girl training to be a nun, or someone without experience (a novice at driving).

20 **d.** *Chanting* = singing, especially on one note as in some churches. *Warbling* and *trilling* = singing on several notes, with a trembling effect (usually of birds). *Chirping* = singing with short sharp notes (usually of birds).

Unit nine

1 **e.** *A frame-up* = a plot to make an innocent person appear guilty. *A cold frame* = a place in the garden where plants or vegetables are grown under a glass cover. *A picture frame* = the wooden or plastic border which holds a picture. *A frame of mind* = a state of mind, a mood.

2 **d.** When people are *harmed, hurt* or *injured*, they can recover. *Wounded* = injured with a weapon.

3 **c.** *A spatula* = a flat-bladed spoon used for spreading paint, etc. *A scoop* = a large, spoon-like tool used for picking up sugar or flour. *A shovel* = a large spade-like tool used for lifting and moving snow, sand, coal or soil.

4 **e.** The nursery rhyme says:

Humpty Dumpty sat on a wall.
Humpty Dumpty had a great fall.
All the king's horses and all the king's men
Couldn't put Humpty together again.

5 **b.** *To gag* = to stop someone speaking by covering the mouth. *To shackle* and *to fetter* = to put chains on people. *Handcuffs* = two rings joined together, placed round the wrists. *To bind* = to tie up.

6 **c.** *Rack and ruin* = (a fixed phrase) a ruined state. *Rubble* = small pieces of broken brick and stone. *A wreck* = a ruined ship. *Neglect* = the state of being uncared for. *Rot* = decay.

7 **b.** *Blood sports* = sports in which animals are killed (bull-fighting, fox-hunting). *Blood donors* = people who give blood for hospitals. *Blood vessels* = tubes in the body which carry the blood. *In cold blood* = unemotionally, without excitement (to kill in cold blood).

8 **d.** *A thoroughfare* = a main public *street* through which traffic flows easily. *A highway* = (old-fashioned) *a main road.*

9 **c.** *A resemblance* = a likeness, similarity. *An image* = an exact copy, likeness (He's the image of his father). *A semblance* = an outward appearance, a suggestion (the semblance of a smile). *A similitude* = (formal) likeness, comparison (the similitude of two triangles).

10 **c.** All these are lists. *A catalogue* = a list of things on view or on sale (a museum catalogue, an auction catalogue). *A register* = a list of people (the voters' register). *An account* = a list of costs, expenses (a bank account). *A tally* = a check list (to keep a tally of your expenses).

11 **d.** *To natter* = to chat. *To converse* = (formal) to have a conversation. *To confer* = (formal) to have a conference, discussion.

12 **a.** *A gill* (a hard 'g' as in 'go') = the opening behind *a fish's* head for breathing; also, a gill (a soft 'g' as in 'gin') = a quarter of a pint. *A fin* = part of a fish used in swimming; also, part of an *aeroplane* tail. *Scales* = the thin plates on a

fish's skin; also, *musical* notes in order; also, a *weighing* machine.

13 **d.** *Humane* = merciful, showing human qualities (a humane action, a humane killer). *Philanthropic* = loving mankind (a philanthropic organisation). *Charitable* = kind, helping people in need (a charitable institution). *Benevolent* = well-wishing, kind (a benevolent old man).

14 **a.** *To snap someone's head off* = to speak suddenly and fiercely to him. *A cold snap* = a sudden spell of cold weather. *A snap election* = an unexpected, sudden election. *A snapshot* = an informal photograph. *A snapdragon* = a garden flower.

15 **a.** *To agitate* something or someone = to shake, to move violently, to excite (people get agitated). All the others = his voice sounded shaky, uncertain.

16 **a.** *Frequent* = happening often (a frequent event). *Renewed* = coming back, perhaps only once (a renewed attack). *Constant* = without a stop (constant pain). *Habitual* = usual, like a habit (a habitual expression, habitual drinking).

17 **e.** *The hind quarters* = the back parts of an animal (the hind legs). *At close quarters* = near to (to inspect something at close quarters). *To ask for quarter* = (old-fashioned) to ask for mercy. *From all quarters* = from all sides. *The lowest quarters* = the least pleasant parts of a town (the residential quarter, business quarter).

18 **b.** The proverb means that you escape from one danger only to fall into another.

19 **d**

20 **c.** (A fixed phrase.) *A mole* = a small furry, underground animal. *A beaver* = a large water animal with a large, flat tail and teeth strong enough to cut down trees. *A rodent* = an animal of the rat family (a mouse, rat, rabbit, beaver).

Unit ten

1 **a.** *A bevy* is not a common word: it usually describes a group of women. We talk about *a clump* of bushes, *a company* of actors.

2 **a**

3 **a.** Also, *to blanch* = to turn pale (of people). *Bleached* = turned white by sunlight or chemicals (bleached material, hair).

4 **c.** We say *the surroundings* (to live in pleasant or ugly surroundings). All the others = nearby, in the surrounding area.

5 **a.** *Bed and breakfast* = accommodation for the night and breakfast, at a moderate price, usually in an ordinary private house. Such notices are very common in seaside resorts. A *bring and buy* sale = a sale of second-hand goods, often in aid of charity.

6 **d.** (A fixed phrase.) *Snug* = safe, warm and cosy.

7 **a.** (An idiom.)

8 **b.** *Risky* = dangerous, but not to describe people (a risky plan, a risky thing to do). *Dauntless* = (literary) brave.

9 **e.** *Catty* is more often applied to women. *Shrewd* = wise, perceptive.

10 **e.** The *big top* = the large, main tent in a circus.

11 **d.** *A dial* = a face with numbers or words on it (as on *radios, telephones, clocks* and *watches*). *A mainspring* = the principal spring in a clock or watch. *A pendulum* = a swinging weight which regulates the movement of a clock.

12 **b.** *As large as life* = (a fixed phrase) in person (I saw him in the street as large as life = it was definitely him I saw).

13 **b.** *Roll call* = the calling of names to check who is present. *A forward roll* = turning head over

heels on the ground. *A roll of honour* = a list of those who have died for their country in war. *A roll of drums* = the sound made when drums are beaten rapidly. *A Swiss roll* = a thin cake spread with jam and rolled up.

14 **c.** (Metaphorical.) *A tether* = (literally) a rope or *chain* for tying up an animal. Dogs wear *a lead* or *a leash*. A boat is fastened to the bank by its *mooring*.

15 **a.** We can feel *dizzy* from turning round and round quickly, sometimes from having too much to drink. *Seedy* = (colloquial) *unwell. Indisposed* = (formal) unwell.

16 **d.** We say: *I'm averse to going*. All the others = I don't want to go.

17 **e.** Doves and pigeons *coo*. Geese *cackle*. *A screech* = a loud, piercing sound or scream (a parrot screeches; the brakes of a car screech when it stops very suddenly). Hens *cluck*.

18 **b.** *A windcheater* and *a windjammer* = an anorak; also, a windjammer = a large sailing ship. *A windfall* = a fruit blown off a tree by the wind; also, an unexpected piece of good luck, especially money. *A wind-break* = a fence or line of trees which breaks the force of the wind.

19 **e.** All the words have a similar meaning, but we never use the others to describe a take-off. *Upright, erect* and *upstanding* = standing up straight; also, upstanding = strong and decent (a fine, upstanding man). *Perpendicular* = at right angles to a surface (perpendicular lines in geometry).

20 **a.** *The first lady* = (US) the wife of the President or a governor of a state. All the words = principal, most important, but the others are unlikely descriptions of ladies.

Unit eleven

1 **e.** Hearing and eyesight may be *acute* (very good), but not eyes. *Spiked* = having a sharp point. *Prickly* = having a lot of small, sharp points (hedgehogs and thistles are prickly). *Barbed* = having a hook-like point, as on a fish-hook.

2 **a.** *The thin end of the wedge* = (an idiom) a small change or demand is likely to lead to bigger changes or demands. *A wedge* = a V-shaped piece of wood or metal used to split things apart.

3 **a**

4 **e.** Rooms or buildings are *vacant* or *unoccupied*. A sheet of paper with nothing on it is *blank*. *Void* = (legal) not valid or binding (of a contract or an agreement).

5 **c.** We never write the others on a letter. *Imperative* and *essential* = (very strong words) extremely important.

6 **c.** *To stagger* = to move along very unsteadily (you stagger if you are in pain or drunk). The others = to walk in a slow, casual way. You usually *ramble* in the country, not along a street (a ramble = a long walk taken for enjoyment).

7 **e.** *A pitchfork* = a fork used to lift hay. *A fork-lift* (truck) = a small vehicle for lifting and lowering goods. *A tuning fork* = a fork which produces a certain note when struck, used for tuning musical instruments. *A fish fork* = a fork used for eating fish. *A trident* = a three-pronged spear like the one carried by Neptune.

8 **c.** (Between two places.) The others have no meaning.

9 **d.** You lose weight or reduce your weight. *To cut the cards* = to divide the pack by lifting a

number of cards off the top, when the pack is lying face downwards. *To cut corners* = to do something quickly and carelessly. *To cut prices* = to lower prices.

10 **b.** *A thicket* = a dense group of bushes or trees. *A posy* and *a nosegay* (not very common) = a small *bunch* of flowers (bridesmaids often carry posies). *A garland* = (old-fashioned) a decorative circle of flowers or leaves.

11 **b.** The others = to pull slowly (a heavy weight). *Towing* is used for boats and road vehicles when they are being pulled along.

12 **e.** *An expectant mother* = (colloquial) a pregnant woman. *Optimistic* and *sanguine* = certain that everything will turn out well in the future.

13 **e.** *Refrigerated* = made cold, as in a refrigerator. *Bleak* = cold and cheerless (bleak weather, a bleak landscape).

14 **c.** (An idiom.) *Blunt* = not bothering to be polite. *Longwinded* = using many words when a few would be sufficient.

15 **e.** *A dentist* works in a surgery. There are different kinds of *studio* (a television studio, a photographic studio, a design studio).

16 **a.** *New issues* = new stamps coming into circulation. Issue = (legal) a child (but we never use it in ordinary conversation). We talk about a particular issue of a newspaper (today's issue of *The Times*).

17 **a.** *Horrified* = very shocked and surprised. *Terrified* and *petrified* = (very strong words) frightened. Petrified = (literally) turned into stone; (metaphorically) too frightened to move.

18 **c.** *To jump out of your skin* = to jump violently (from a shock or surprise). *To jump a queue* = to join a queue near the front instead of at the end.

To jump down someone's throat = to speak sharply to someone. *To jump at an idea* = to accept an idea eagerly. *To jump to it* = to do something promptly.

19 **e.** *A full stop* = . *A comma* = , *A hyphen* = - (as in Anglo-French). *A semicolon* = ; *A colon* = :

20 **a.** *Sturdy* = strong, solidly built (children, animals, furniture). *Potent* = powerful (alcoholic drink, medicine). *Stout* = strong, or brave, or fat. *Mighty* = powerful (a mighty king, a mighty blow).

Unit twelve

1 **b**

2 **e.** *A resident, an inhabitant* and *a dweller* = people who live in a place (but were not necessarily born there). *An aboriginal* = (very unusual) a member of a country's earliest, most primitive race. When we talk about aborigines we usually mean Australian Aborigines.

3 **d.** (A fixed phrase.) *Nooks* and *crannies* = small, secret corners where things might be hidden. *An ingle* = (very unusual) a fire, or fireplace, but notice: an inglenook = the chimney-corner in an old-fashioned fireplace, considered rather picturesque these days. *A chink* = a narrow opening, a crack.

4 **a.** *Sensitive* = delicate, easily affected. A sensitive *film* is affected by exposure to light. A sensitive *artist* is capable of very delicate expression. A sensitive person is easily upset.

5 **a.** All the other words = close (but are not followed by 'for'). *Intimate* = personal, private (an intimate friendship is a very close one). *Neighbouring* and *adjacent* = next to (the

neighbouring house, the adjacent street). *Nigh* = (old-fashioned) near.

6 **b.** We could say: Is it *probable* (likely) or *conceivable* (imaginable) that a man could swim the Channel? *Workable* = something that will work, be effective (a plan, an arrangement); we don't say: Is it workable to do that? *Capable* = able (a capable person, a car capable of reaching 100 m.p.h.).

7 **d.** c/o = *care of*; we write it on the envelope of a letter sent to a person staying at someone else's house (Mr J. Smith, c/o Mrs E. Jones). CO = *Commanding Officer*. Co. = *Company*.

8 **b.** *A caricature* = a distorted or exaggerated drawing of a person. *A parody* = a humorous *imitation* (especially of an author's style of writing). *A counterfeit* = an imitation made to deceive (counterfeit banknotes). *An image* = a likeness (a wooden image of a saint, the image of yourself you see in a mirror, a mental image of someone you have never seen).

9 **a.** We *transport* things like goods and freight. *To convey, to transmit* and *to deliver* a message = to pass on a message. *To bear* a message = to carry a message.

10 **b.** *To drop off* = to fall asleep. *To drop a brick* = (colloquial) to make a blunder. *To drop in* = to call in (at someone's house, or office). *To drop someone a line* = (colloquial) to write someone a letter. *To drop through* = to fall through (the chimney dropped through the roof).

11 **d.** *A banknote* = paper money (a £5 note, a £10 note). *A receipt* = a slip of paper acknowledging payment. *A check* = a type of receipt (often a disc or piece of paper you get when you leave your coat in a cloakroom). *A cheque* (US check) = a printed slip which orders the bank

to pay out money. If you save money in a bank, it is kept in your *account*. In Britain, *a bill* = a written statement of charges (a gas or electricity bill, the bill in a restaurant).

12 **c.** We don't use the others for a clock. We talk about a *true* friend, a true account; a *genuine* excuse, a genuine or *authentic* work of art (not a copy). *Unerring* = completely accurate (the unerring aim of a marksman).

13 **d.** The proverb means that people prefer the company of those who have the same tastes and interests as themselves.

14 **a.** *A brook* = a small stream. *Babbling* = the gentle sound of water flowing over stones. Leaves moving in the wind *rustle*. Silky material makes a *swishing* sound as it moves. A very small bell *tinkles*. Raindrops *patter* on the window; small children's feet patter on the ground.

15 **a.** We never say the others. He was *submerging*, he was *sinking* = he was going down (often in water), but we never say: I submerged him, or, I sank him. When an unsuccessful business is *liquidated*, it stops operating and is sold up to pay off debts. We *water* plants, not people.

16 **b**

17 **c.** *A slit* = a long, narrow opening (a tear in clothing, a letter-box slit). Slits are usually man-made. The other words = *cracks* or openings (usually in rocks or in the ground).

18 **c.** *To reel in* = to wind the line round the reel at the end of a fishing rod. *To reel off* = to say something rapidly and fluently. *To reel from side to side* = to stagger about. *A reel of cotton* = a small cylinder for holding cotton (it is sold on a reel).

19 **d.** *A fault* and *a defect* = something wrong (with a machine, a piece of equipment, or a

person's character or actions). *A vice* = a serious bad habit (drinking, gambling). *A sin* = (religious) a moral crime.

20 **c**

Unit thirteen

1 **e.** *A swindler* = someone who cheats others out of their money.

2 **e.** All five words = the highest point. We talk about the *summit* of a mountain; the *crest* of a hill, or a wave; the *zenith* of someone's career (the sun at its zenith is directly overhead); the *climax* of an exciting story, or a quarrel.

3 **e.** All the others = the year after the one in question. To be *consecutive* things must be plural: three consecutive years = three years which follow one after the other.

4 **b.** You might feel all the other emotions, but *condolences* are the expression of sympathy.

5 **e.** *Callous* = hard, unfeeling.

6 **d.** *Hale and hearty* = (a fixed phrase) strong and healthy (especially of old people).

7 **b.** A nail file = an instrument for smoothing the fingernails; we don't say *nail filings*. *Iron filings* = small, fine pieces of iron removed with a file. *A filing cabinet* = a box or set of drawers for keeping letters and papers. *In single file* = in a line, one behind another. *A filing clerk* = someone whose job it is to keep papers in order in filing cabinets (to file papers).

8 **e.** All these are different signs. *A symptom* = the sign of an illness (a temperature, a sore throat are symptoms). *A symbol* = a sign representing something (+, −, ×, ÷ are mathematical symbols; the cross is the symbol of Christianity). *A clue* = anything that helps to solve a mystery, a problem (detectives look for

clues). *A hint* = an indirect sign or suggestion (to drop someone a hint). *An emblem* = a sign representing something, especially an ornamental device or badge (on a flag or shield).

9 **d.** (Wit = quickness of mind.) *Droll* = amusing and also slightly odd (less common than the other words).

10 **e.** *Potato crisps* (usually just *crisps*) = thin slices of potato, fried, dried and sold in packets. *Baked potatoes* = potatoes cooked in the oven. *French fried* (US) = *chips* (but now often used in Britain). *Potato croquettes* = potatoes covered in breadcrumbs and cooked in fat.

11 **d.** *A pipeline* = a long pipe, sometimes underground, for carrying oil or gas. *Pipe down!* = Be quiet! *A windpipe* = a tube in the body which takes air to the lungs. *A blowpipe* = a pipe for blowing air on to a flame to increase heat; also, a long tube for firing arrows or darts with the breath, used by primitive people.

12 **e.** A *genuine* signature = a signature actually written by its owner and not an imitation written by someone else. A *correct* signature = a signature written without mistakes. It would be unusual to use the other words to describe a signature.

13 **e.** *A pane* = a sheet of glass. *A sash cord* = a strong cord to hold up a sash window (a window with a frame that slides up and down). *A sill* = a narrow shelf at the bottom of a window.

14 **c.** British Medical Association (B.M.A.). All the words = groups of people with a common interest.

15 **b.** *A slope, an incline* and *a slant* = a surface or line which is at an angle, not flat (the slope of a hillside, or a river bank; a steep incline; the

slant of a roof, or of the sun's rays). *The gradient* = the degree of slope (a hill with a one in six gradient = a hill which rises one metre in every six).

16 **a.** (A man of large or small *stature*.) *Altitude* = height (of mountains, aeroplanes). *Highness* = the title given to royalty (Her Royal Highness, Queen Elizabeth). *Elevation* = raising to a higher place (a person's elevation to a more important job); also, an elevation = a high point (an elevation 3000 metres above sea level). *Eminence* = fame, distinction.

17 **e.** The proverb means it is wisest to be honest. All the words = *a plan* on which to base your actions. A government or a business company follow certain *policies*. We talk about housing *schemes*, irrigation schemes, colour schemes; a military *strategy* (especially the positioning of troops). *Practice* = actions you perform habitually (It is my practice to write my diary every day).

18 **d.** To say something *tongue-in-cheek* = to say something ironically and not seriously.

19 **e.** *A dormer window* = an upright window set in a sloping roof. *Bay* and *bow windows* both jut out beyond the wall of a building to make extra space in the room inside: a bay window usually has three sides, a bow window is curved. *A French window* = a glass door (usually into a garden). *A casement* = (uncommon) an ordinary window you push outwards to open.

20 **e.** (Usually of a slow-moving river.) The others are similar movements. *Contorts* is like *twists* but suggests a more violent movement (a face contorted with rage). A snake *coils* itself round you. A wheatfield *undulates* or ripples in the wind.

Unit fourteen

1 **d.** (It usually describes a child.) *A gossip column* = a regular, informal newspaper article talking about well-known people and social events.

2 **b.** *Turquoise* = greenish blue (the colour of the stone). A fawn is a young deer, and so from this, *fawn* = a light yellowish brown. *Indigo* = deep violet blue.

3 **c.** *To fry* eggs = to cook eggs in fat. *To boil* = to cook in boiling water (eggs in their shells). *To scramble* eggs = to cook beaten eggs with milk and butter until they thicken. *To poach* eggs = to cook eggs without their shells in boiling water. *To bake* = to cook in the oven (cakes, bread). *To stew* = to cook slowly in liquid. *To steam* = to cook in steam (puddings). *To broil* = to roast. *To grill* = to cook on metal bars above a fire, or under the grill of a cooker.

4 **c.** *To slacken* = to make loose. *To untie* and *to unloose* = to undo (knots, rope, string or someone who is tied up). *To liberate* and *to release* = to set free (we liberate prisoners, oppressed people; we release people, animals, gases, information).

5 **b.** *Tidings* = (old-fashioned) news. *A bulletin* = an official news *report. A news flash* = a brief report on something important which has just happened.

6 **e.** *A fridge* = a refrigerator. *A cold store* = a large, refrigerated room, usually for keeping food. *A deep freeze* = a large, domestic container cold enough to preserve food for a long time. *A freezer* = the freezing compartment of an ordinary fridge or deep freeze. *A cooler* = any container that keeps things cool; also (slang), gaol.

7 **c.** The other four = narrow channels. *Ditches* are found in the countryside, usually for drainage. *Drains, gullies* (or gulleys) and *gutters* are all parts of the drainage system of streets and buildings.

8 **c.** *To beat about the bush* = (an idiom) to approach a subject in an indirect way. Don't beat about the bush = Come to the point.

9 **a.** All five describe things which make you laugh, but something *absurd* or *ridiculous* would cause mocking laughter rather than simple amusement. *Hilarious* = extremely funny.

10 **e.** *Law-abiding* = not breaking the law. All the others describe a friend you can trust and rely on.

11 **c.** The other four suggest an orderly assembly. A *swarming* crowd suggests many people moving about restlessly (bees, flies, ants swarm).

12 **b.** *A candidate* = someone who offers himself for a particular office (especially in parliamentary elections). *An applicant* = a person who asks for something (for a job, for a loan). *A claimant* = someone who makes a claim (a claim for damages or compensation in a law court; a claim to a title, a throne). *An opponent* = someone you fight or compete against (a boxer, a person who disagrees with you, or a person you play against in chess, bridge, etc).

13 **a.** To board a ship you go up *a gangway*. *A walkway* = (unusual) a road or path for pedestrians only.

14 **d.** *An extraction* = the removal of a tooth. *A filling* = something which is put into a tooth to repair it. *To drill* = to make a hole in a tooth in order to put in a filling. Drills are used for many purposes, including mining, road-building and woodwork.

15 **a.** *To play truant* = to be away from school without permission. *To play the fool* = to be

deliberately silly. *To play the game* = to be fair. *To play second fiddle* = to take a subordinate role. *To play to the gallery* = to seek popular applause.

16 **b**

17 **c.** In England, the education of 5 to 11 year old children = *primary education. The Prime Minister* = the leading minister in a government. *Prime beef* = top quality beef. *A prime number* = a number which can only be divided by itself or 1 (5, 7, 11). *Prime cost* = the cost of production, not taking profit or overheads into account.

18 **d.** A gramophone record is an example of *a disc*. *A bulb* = an electric light bulb; also, the root of some plants (daffodils grow from bulbs). *Globes, spheres* and *orbs* are all shaped like a ball, and are similar in meaning: we call the Earth a globe (but it also has a spherical shape); the planets are spheres; orb is often used in a poetic sense.

19 **b.** *Point-blank range* = very close range (so that it is impossible to miss the target). *A point of honour* = any matter about which you have strong feelings of duty or obligation. *A turning point* = a critical, decisive moment (in a career, in history). *To come to the point* = to say what is essential. *A point of view* = an opinion.

20 **b.** Bats = (slang) crazy.

Unit fifteen

1 **a.** The *upper classes* = the aristocracy. *Upper ranks* = people in high places (the upper ranks of the army). *First grade* = of the best quality. Notice: first grade = (US) the first year class at school. *Primary stages* = the early period (of growth, development).

2 **e.** *As sober as a judge* = (a fixed phrase) very serious, not drunk. *Barristers, solicitors* and *lawyers* = members of the legal profession. *A juror* = a member of the public serving on a jury in a court of law.

3 **a.** All five have the sense of going round, but only *a revolution* = one complete turn. We talk about *a twist* or *a turn* in a road when it goes round a corner. *Circulation* = movement (of the blood round the body, or of road traffic, or of crowds of people). *Rotation* = movement (of machinery; crop rotation = the movement of crops from field to field in a definite order).

4 **a.** A public house with this sign is not owned by a brewery and therefore it may sell a variety of beers. The tendency is for breweries to buy up free houses and consequently their number is growing smaller.

5 **b.** (An idiom.) *A bonnet* = a woman's hat with strings which tie under the chin; bonnets are no longer worn and now the word is not often used in this sense; also, a bonnet = the engine cover of a motor car.

6 **a.** *To measure your length* = to fall flat on the ground. The other words all have something to do with length and distance but are wrong here.

7 **a.** (We also use the word power in this sense.) *Potential* = the possibilities of a situation, or what a person may be capable of. *Vigour* = energy, activity (of people). *Force* often has the meaning of violence: if we enter a house by force, we might break down the door; also, we talk about the force of the wind, of an argument, of a blow.

8 **e.** Precious stones are *cut* and *polished* before they are used in jewellery. *Setting* = the metal framework which holds them in a necklace or bracelet.

9 **b.** *Twin track* = having two recording tracks on each side of the tape. *A running track* is found on a sports field. We say someone has *a one-track mind* if he keeps returning to the same subject. *To track down* = to find after a long and thorough search. *To cover up your tracks* = (metaphorically) to conceal where you have been or what you have done.

10 **d.** All the others describe careful, thorough people, but only *punctual* refers to time-keeping.

11 **b.** (Colloquial.)

12 **e.** *Buff* = a light yellow colour. *Tawny* = yellowish brown. *Sandy* = yellowish red.

13 **d.** *Bellowing* = a very loud noise, showing either amusement or anger (often used for the roar of a bull). *Tittering, giggling* and *chuckling* = quiet, suppressed laughter (tittering often suggests mocking laughter). *Cackling* = loud, harsh laughter.

14 **c.** *An arrow* is fired with a bow. *A harpoon* = the weapon used to kill whales. Throwing the *javelin* is a sport. *Spears* and *darts* = primitive weapons; also, darts = a game, often played in pubs.

15 **e.** *A spot* is the other word which describes a blemish on the skin. *A speck* = a tiny particle (a speck of dirt). *A flaw* = a blemish, a defect (in a jewel, an argument, someone's character). *A smudge* = a mark made when something is rubbed or smeared (a smudge of dirt or ink).

16 **c.** Notice: *a log fire* crackles; *roasting meat* sizzles; *a loose floorboard* creaks; *a vacuum cleaner* hums.

17 **c.** *Scum* = dirty froth on the surface of water. *Froth* = a collection of small bubbles, foam (usually found on top of drinks; on beer, coffee). *Spray* = tiny drops of water blown by the wind. *Spume* = foam which appears on the

sea. *Lather* = a frothy mixture of soap and water.

18 **a.** (A fixed phrase.) *A rough and tumble* = a struggle or fight.

19 **a.** (The water is coming over the top.) Things *leak* if they have a hole through which the liquid escapes. Babies *dribble* when saliva runs out of their mouths.

20 **b.** *A tale* = a story (usually short). *A narrative* = a description (often quite long) of a series of events. *An account* = any kind of descriptive report (often factual as in an account of an accident, a journey). *A legend* = a traditional story which is not necessarily true (the stories of King Arthur and the Knights of the Round Table are legends).

Ihr Testergebnis

Unit one	11
Unit two	
Unit three	
Unit four	
Unit five	
Unit six	
Unit seven	
Unit eight	
Unit nine	
Unit ten	
Unit eleven	
Unit twelve	
Unit thirteen	
Unit fourteen	
Unit fifteen	
GESAMT	

Wie geht es weiter?

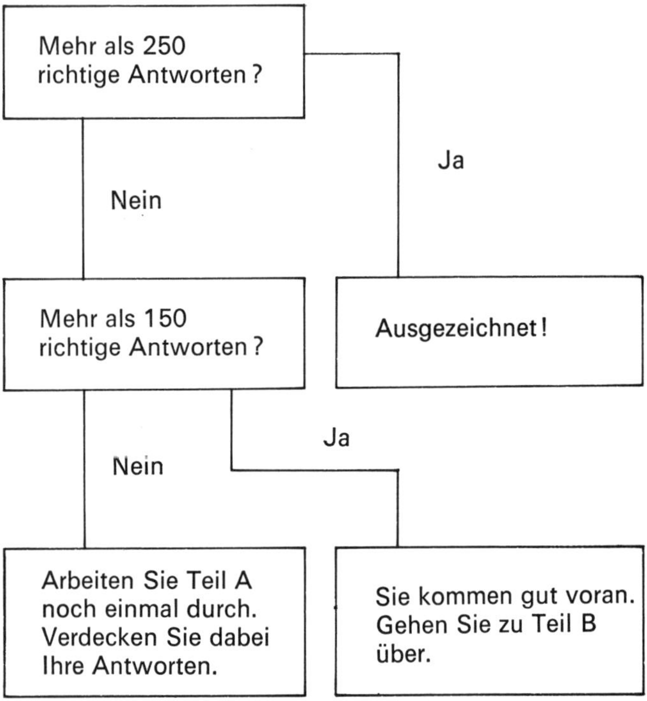

TEIL B

Unit one

1 Which do you see at a tennis match?
a. an examiner
b. an umpire
c. an adjudicator
d. a judge
e. a referee

2 All these words, except one, describe the weather.
a. sultry
b. close
c. sweltering
d. torrid
e. molten

3 You might listen to exciting news with bated
a. eyes
b. breath
c. heart
d. blood
e. feelings

4 The opposite of *temporary* is
a. everlasting
b. habitual
c. permanent
d. established
e. persistent

5 When you buy a gramophone record, it is in
a. a sheath
b. an envelope
c. a bag
d. a wallet
e. a sleeve

6 A rather rude way of describing a thin person is *all . . . and bones.*
a. sinew d. flesh
b. muscle e. gristle
c. skin

7 Your solicitor is your
a. lawful adviser
b. legal adviser
c. legitimate adviser
d. authorised adviser
e. legalised adviser

8 Which phrase goes with the picture?
a. keeping his head above water
b. keeping a straight face
c. keeping his head
d. keeping up appearances
e. keeping up with the Joneses

9 Another word for *building* a house is
a. making d. constructing
b. manufacturing e. producing
c. composing

10 Which man is tired?
a. He strode along the street.
b. He strutted along the street.
c. He trudged along the street.
d. He ambled along the street.
e. He stalked along the street.

11 These all mean the same thing, but which one would you not see on a public notice?
a. loo
b. lavatory
c. toilet
d. WC
e. washroom

12 Sap is the moisture inside plants and trees. What is a sapling?
a. an instrument for extracting sap
b. a flower
c. an insect which lives on sap
d. a wise man
e. a young tree

13 Four of these words have something to do with hearing or listening. Which one is different?
a. an audition
b. audible
c. an auditorium
d. audacious
e. an audience

14 Which of these is the most friendly?
a. an argument
b. a discussion
c. a dispute
d. a contradiction
e. a controversy

15 Finish this phrase: as light as
a. plumage
b. a plume
c. a quill
d. down
e. a feather

16 The words *transept, altar* and *pew* all have something to do with
a. churches
b. printing
c. transport
d. the cinema
e. corrections

17 Which word means *extremely happy*?
a. cheerful
b. genial
c. elated
d. sprightly
e. blithe

18 Finish this proverb: Two wrongs don't make a
a. lawful
b. true
c. right
d. correct
e. fair

19 What is this?
a. a bull in a china shop
b. a bulldozer
c. a bullring
d. a bull's-eye
e. a bulldog

20 Which can you not call *an image?*
a. an idea
b. a piece of music
c. an idol
d. a reflection in a mirror
e. a close similarity

Unit two

1 All British people know that Old King Cole was
a. the English poet, S. T. Coleridge
b. a merry old soul
c. a pop group
d. King of England in 1066
e. a rich miner

2 Which of these is wrong?
a. I shan't be a minute.
b. I shan't be a moment.
c. I shan't be a tick.
d. I shan't be a second.
e. I shan't be a twinkling.

3 When a child is well behaved, you say he is *as good as*
a. gold
b. copper
c. silver
d. brass
e. steel

4 All the following, except one, are ways of saying *to die*. Which one means something else?
a. to hold your breath
b. to pass away
c. to breathe your last
d. to peg out
e. to end your days

☐

5 The words *noun, subject* and *negative* all have something to do with
a. nationality
b. printing
c. grammar
d. names
e. photography

☐

6 Which is the least polite way of telling someone you don't believe him?
a. I don't believe you.
b. That's hard to believe.
c. Nonsense!
d. You're a liar!
e. That's not true.

☐

7 Which phrase goes with the picture on the next page?
a. goose-flesh
b. a gooseberry fool
c. playing gooseberry
d. goose-step
e. a wild goose chase

☐

8 Which is wrong?
a. refined petrol
b. refined sugar
c. refined speech
d. refined water
e. refined manners

9 In a restaurant you
a. give an order to the waiter
b. command the waiter
c. instruct the waiter
d. dictate to the waiter
e. direct the waiter

10 If someone gave you a short and rather impolite answer, you would say he was
a. curt
b. brief
c. abbreviated
d. little
e. concise

11 Finish this proverb: Discretion is the better part of
a. boldness
b. gallantry
c. courage
d. valour
e. bravery

12 An American says *an overpass* when an Englishman says
a. a bridge
b. a flyover
c. a crossing
d. a viaduct
e. a junction

13 An unbreakable rule is a hard and . . . rule.
a. swift
b. quick
c. fast
d. solid
e. firm

14 When you put in for a new job, you are
a. a competitor
b. a claimant
c. an opponent
d. an applicant
e. a rival

15 If your shoe is too small you might say it
a. presses
b. squashes
c. nips
d. pinches
e. squeezes

16 All these are kinds of rebellion, but which one can be peaceful?
a. a mutiny
b. a revolution
c. a riot
d. a demonstration
e. an insurrection

17 *Parent* is to *child* as *guardian* is to
- a. child
- b. ward
- c. grandchild
- d. twin
- e. foster child

18 The parts of a wheel which join the middle to the outside edge are the
- a. rays
- b. spokes
- c. radii
- d. bars
- e. joiners

19 Which phrase goes with the picture?
- a. putting in an appearance
- b. putting his foot down
- c. putting two and two together
- d. putting his foot in it
- e. putting him off his stroke

20 Which of these is wrong?
- a. Your life is in threat.
- b. Your life is in danger.
- c. Your life is in peril.
- d. Your life is in jeopardy.
- e. Your life is at risk.

Unit three

1 A highbrow is
a. the top of a hill
b. an intellectual
c. a bald man
d. the line of hair above the eye
e. the forehead

☐

2 Your nearest relation is
a. your closest kin
b. your first kin
c. your kinnest
d. your next of kin
e. your next kin

☐

3 When an Englishman wants a whisky with nothing added, he orders it neat. An American asks for it
a. with ginger
b. with soda
c. long
d. on the rocks
e. straight

☐

4 Which of these does not have the meaning of *escaping*?
a. fleeing
b. absconding
c. avoiding
d. departing
e. retreating

☐

5 Which is wrong?
- a. I'm boiling with anger.
- b. I'm fuming with anger.
- c. I'm simmering with anger.
- d. I'm blazing with anger.
- e. I'm cooking with anger.

6 Which of these is not part of your clothing?
- a. a brim
- b. a turn-up
- c. a hat trick
- d. a lapel
- e. a vent

7 Which man draws plans?
- a. an artist
- b. a cartoonist
- c. an engraver
- d. a draughtsman
- e. a caricaturist

8 When someone says: *I took it with a pinch of salt,* he is
- a. cooking
- b. taking medicine
- c. showing disbelief
- d. cleaning his teeth
- e. superstitious

9 Which of these is a formal word meaning *a friend*?
a. a pal
b. a comrade
c. a chum
d. a buddy
e. an ally

10 What does a mother sing to her baby to send it to sleep?
a. a hymn
b. a carol
c. a chant
d. a lullaby
e. a dirge

11 Which person pays rent?
a. an owner
b. a possessor
c. an occupant
d. a proprietor
e. a tenant

12 All these words mean *mad*, but which one cannot be used to describe an idea?
a. crazy
b. insane
c. deranged
d. lunatic
e. daft

13 Finish this proverb: You can't teach an . . . dog new tricks.
a. old
b. antique
c. elderly
d. ancient
e. aged

14 Which phrase goes with the picture?
a. a hundred to one the rest
b. laid to rest
c. rest assured
d. rest on your oars
e. rest on your laurels

15 If you stick a knife into someone, you
a. stab him
b. puncture him
c. perforate him
d. drill him
e. bore him

16 If someone was amused for a very short time, we would say his amusement was
a. provisional
b. shortlived
c. impermanent
d. extemporary
e. transient

17 You could describe a haughty man as high and
a. powerful
b. strong
c. mighty
d. exalted
e. revered

18 Which of these is not a club?
a. the weapon carried by British policemen
b. a heavy stick used as a weapon
c. a stick used in golf
d. a society
e. a black, leaf-like design on playing cards

19 Which phrase goes with the picture?
a. leading him a dance
b. leading him by the nose
c. a juvenile lead
d. leading a double life
e. taking the lead

20 The words *junction, points* and *cutting* all have something to do with
a. railways
b. cooking
c. examinations
d. rivers
e. roads

Unit four

1 Choose the right order for these parts of the leg, starting from the foot?
a. ankle, shin, calf, knee, thigh
b. thigh, knee, calf, shin, ankle
c. ankle, calf, shin, thigh, knee
d. ankle, knee, shin, calf, thigh
e. shin, ankle, calf, knee, thigh

2 Which of these does not mean *lazy*?
a. indolent
b. dormant
c. idle
d. slothful
e. lackadaisical

3 Which of these is wrong?
a. a charge of theft
b. a shoulder charge
c. hotel charges
d. school charges
e. an electrical charge

4 Which man would you least like to meet?
a. a robust man
b. an energetic man
c. a forceful man
d. a violent man
e. a vigorous man

5 If you send a parcel through the post and there is glass inside, what do you write on it?
a. Feeble!
b. Fragile!
c. Weak!
d. Impotent!
e. Frail!

6 Which phrase goes with the picture?
a. wearing oilskins
b. burning the midnight oil
c. a study in oils
d. pouring oil on troubled waters
e. oiling his palm

7 Which of these bushes does not have thorns?
a. briar
b. hawthorn
c. gorse
d. laurel
e. rose

8 Which word usually completes this phrase: cloak and
a. sword
b. gown
c. doublet
d. breeches
e. dagger

9 Which of these has a different meaning from the others?
a. to infringe the law
b. to overstep the law
c. to violate the law
d. to break the law
e. to pass the law

☐

10 Which of these do we never say?
a. The engine was chugging.
b. The engine was throbbing.
c. The engine was spluttering.
d. The engine was jangling.
e. The engine was purring.

☐

11 The words *perforation*, *watermark* and *sheet* all have something to do with
a. stamps
b. sailing
c. banknotes
d. printing
e. washing

☐

12 If the work you do becomes unnecessary, your employer may make you
a. superfluous
b. abundant
c. redundant
d. surplus
e. excessive

☐

13 *Lord* and *Sir* are English
a. headings
b. nicknames
c. surnames
d. captions
e. titles

☐

14 Men who are brave because they have been drinking alcohol have got . . . courage.

a. American
b. Russian
c. Dutch
d. French
e. German

15 What would be most likely to make a blaring sound?

a. a breeze
b. a trumpet
c. a revolver
d. a blizzard
e. an electric drill

16 Which of these is nearest in meaning to *to put up with*?

a. to tolerate
b. to authorise
c. to sanction
d. to permit
e. to allow

17 If you crow about something, what are you doing?

a. singing
b. exulting
c. apologising
d. whispering
e. crying

18 If you are feeling nervous about a task that must be done, you have to . . . up courage.

a. pick
b. pluck
c. pull
d. jerk
e. snatch

19 Which phrase goes with the picture?
a. the down train
b. a trainee
c. in training
d. a train of thought
e. a train-bearer

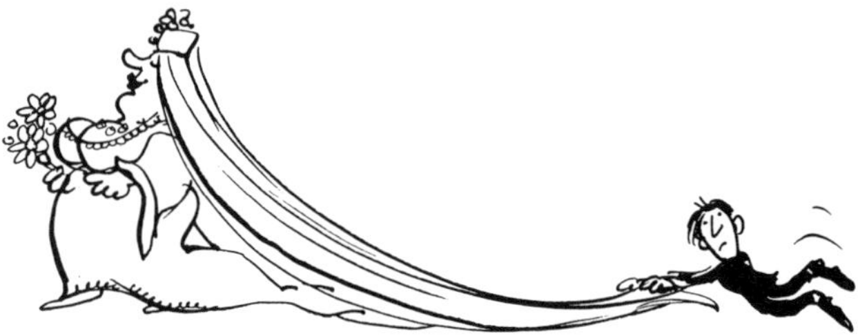

20 An American says *a truck* when an Englishman says
a. a car
b. a van
c. a lorry
d. a wagon
e. a trailer

Unit five

1 Which of these is not a hat?
a. a bowler
b. a muffler
c. a trilby
d. a beret
e. a deerstalker

2 The two holes in the nose are
a. nostrils
b. chimneys
c. ventilators
d. funnels
e. shafts

☐

3 Which of these is wrong?
a. ruined pencils
b. ruined hopes
c. ruined buildings
d. ruined health
e. ruined children

☐

4 Which would you do in horror and disgust?
a. retreat
b. recede
c. withdraw
d. recoil
e. rebound

☐

5 Finish this proverb: Familiarity . . . contempt.
a. generates
b. breeds
c. begets
d. rears
e. produces

☐

6 Which of these words does not mean *trouble*?
a. an occurrence
b. a disorder
c. a crisis
d. an accident
e. an emergency

☐

7 Which of these is smallest?
a. a pebble
b. a rock
c. a stone
d. a crag
e. a cliff

☐

8 If you buy something and sell it for a higher price, the extra money is your
a. income
b. winnings
c. profit
d. salary
e. acquisition

9 Which of these is not a bow?
a. a part of the circumference of a circle
b. a weapon for shooting arrows
c. the stick used by a violinist
d. a knot of ribbon
e. the front end of a ship

10 Complete this phrase: to all intents and
a. intentions
b. purposes
c. propositions
d. meanings
e. designs

11 When you put things in a list, showing which ones you like best, it is your order of
a. preference
b. alternative
c. selection
d. decision
e. option

12 These mean the same, but which usually has a religious meaning?
a. a law
b. a rule
c. a commandment
d. an order
e. a regulation

13 Which of these can you do without using words?
a. praise someone
b. commend someone
c. compliment someone
d. flatter someone
e. applaud someone

14 Which answer goes with the picture?
a. a stepson
b. step this way
c. out of step
d. step by step
e. stepping stones

15 Which of these does not mean *a rich man*?
a. a wealthy man
b. an expensive man
c. an affluent man
d. a monied man
e. a well-to-do man

16 An American talks about the *hood* of his car when an Englishman talks about
a. the roof
b. the bonnet
c. the radiator
d. the wing
e. the boot

17 Which means the same as *on second thoughts*?
a. second sight
b. on reflection
c. in arrears
d. another point of view
e. in retrospect

18 Cookers, refrigerators and dish-washers are kitchen
a. equipment
b. gear
c. tackle
d. apparatus
e. machinery

19 Which answer goes with the picture?
a. marked down
b. a birthmark
c. marking time
d. make your mark
e. a marked man

20 Which of these fruits is a different colour from the others?
a. a blackcurrant
b. a prune
c. a damson
d. a gooseberry
e. a sloe

Unit six

1 The first letters of your names are your
a. beginners
b. starters
c. initials
d. primaries
e. maidens

2 One of the words in the plural is wrong. Which is it?
a. waitress, waitresses
b. glass, glasses
c. gas, gasses
d. success, successes
e. goose, geese

3 What is the word for the metal wire inside an electric light bulb?
a. the fibre
b. the filament
c. the stripe
d. the strip
e. the line

4 All these are sounds we make when we are amused: which is the loudest?
a. a giggle
b. a laugh
c. a titter
d. a guffaw
e. a chuckle

5 Which of these is not a crop?
a. plants growing in a field
b. a sudden occurrence
c. a very short haircut
d. the handle of a whip
e. part of a bird's throat

☐

6 The most exciting part of a story is its
a. peak
b. climax
c. top
d. summit
e. crown

☐

7 Two people of completely opposite character are as different as
a. bread and cheese
b. cream and cheese
c. wine and cheese
d. chalk and cheese
e. cheese and pickles

☐

8 When your work is much too difficult, you feel out of your
a. mind
b. element
c. class
d. depth
e. senses

☐

9 An old maid is a rather derogatory description for
a. a virgin
b. a widow
c. a damsel
d. a single girl
e. a spinster

☐

10 Which of these is most likely to be a sign of pain?

a. a smile
b. a snigger
c. a grin
d. a smirk
e. a grimace

11 Which of these is a place where a river meets the sea?

a. a gulf
b. a bay
c. an estuary
d. an inlet
e. a cove

12 Which of these do people not wear round their waists?

a. a stole
b. a cummerbund
c a girdle
d. a belt
e. a sash

13 We park a car, but what do we do to a boat?

a. lodge it
b. pitch it
c deposit it
d. moor it
e. park it

14 What is this?

a. an outline
b. a silhouette
c. a profile
d. a contour
e. a cross-section

15 Which person is a botanist?
- a. He classified the flowers.
- b. He ordered the flowers.
- c. He arranged the flowers.
- d. He grouped the flowers.
- e. He divided the flowers.

16 Which word describes the way a sick person walks?
- a. slowly
- b. languidly
- c. gently
- d. unhurriedly
- e. leisurely

17 An American says *a freight car* when an Englishman says
- a. a locomotive
- b. a tender
- c. a goods van
- d. a pullman
- e. a guard's van

18 Which answer goes with the picture?
- a. in the stocks
- b. a laughing stock
- c. stocks and shares
- d. livestock
- e. stock-taking

19 Finish this saying: First come, first
a. helped
b. assisted
c. aided
d. served
e. dealt with

20 What does wood do when it gets wet?
a. it inflates
b. it extends
c. it increases
d. it swells
e. it grows

Unit seven

1 Which movement is the most violent?
a. to cast
b. to pitch
c. to hurl
d. to throw
e. to toss

2 Which speaker is not protesting?
a. I'm innocent
b. I'm harmless
c. I'm guiltless
d. I'm blameless
e. I'm naive

3 When a mother holds a baby in her arms, she is
a. supporting it
b. sustaining it
c. bearing it
d. maintaining it
e. cradling it

4 Which means something different?
a. She challenged me to come.
b. She begged me to come.
c. She entreated me to come.
d. She implored me to come.
e. She pleaded with me to come.

5 If a man lived forever he would be
a. ceaseless
b. never-ending
c. everlasting
d. immortal
e. undying

6 Which phrase goes with the picture?
a. on the wing
b. waiting in the wings
c. the east wing
d. take under your wing
e. a wing chair

7 A hole in a tooth is

a. a cavity
b. a dent
c. a recess
d. a cave
e. a dimple

8 Which word usually completes this phrase: without rhyme or

a. reason
b. poetry
c. verse
d. mime
e. cause

9 What sound does an elephant make?

a. it roars
b. it brays
c. it snarls
d. it growls
e. it trumpets

10 A free-for-all is

a. a shop which charges its customers nothing
b. a fight or argument that anyone can join in
c. a restaurant where the food is free
d. a jumble sale
e. a charitable institution

11 Which of these means *to think very deeply*?

a. to consider
b. to meditate
c. to reflect
d. to dream
e. to ponder

12 Finish this proverb: Many hands make light
a. duty
b. trouble
c. toil
d. labour
e. work

13 When no one has grown anything in a piece of ground, it is
a. green soil
b. mint soil
c. unused soil
d. virgin soil
e. new soil

14 An American says *a wrench* when an Englishman says
a. a spanner
b. a vice
c. a chisel
d. a hammer
e. a screwdriver

15 The words *tide*, *swell* and *plankton*, all have something to do with
a. time
b. the sea
c. illness
d. food
e. string

16 Which is correct?
a. a proposal of marriage
b. a tender of marriage
c. a bid of marriage
d. a proposition of marriage
e. an invitation of marriage

17 Which phrase goes with the picture?
a. a pair of scales
b. a minor scale
c. drawn to scale
d. turning the scales
e. on a small scale

18 Which do we use to describe a rather fat person?
a. round
b. rotund
c. circular
d. spherical
e. oval

19 Finish this phrase: as right as
a. fog
b. sleet
c. rain
d. hail
e. snow

20 All these are drawings or paintings, but which one is done in the shortest time?
a. a sketch
b. a portrait
c. a miniature
d. a cartoon
e. a study

Unit eight

1 Which of these is wrong?
a. a rocking horse
b. a clothes horse
c. a vaulting horse
d. a racehorse
e. a riding horse

2 *Offspring* means
a. a jump
b. the end of the spring season
c. part of a watch
d. a child
e. a branch of a stream

3 Which man may be ill?
a. He spoke heatedly.
b. He spoke feverishly.
c. He spoke warmly.
d. He spoke fervently.
e. He spoke ardently.

4 The opposite of *to accept* is
a. to reject
b. to repulse
c. to retort
d. to rejoin
e. to rescind

5 When you paint something again, you put on a second
a. layer
b. cover
c. stratum
d. thickness
e. coat

6 What is a wet blanket?
a. a discouraging person
b. an overcast sky
c. a thick bank of fog
d. a waterproof cape for cyclists
e. a waterproof blanket for camping

7 Complete this phrase: fame and
a. renown
b. prestige
c. the famous
d. celebrity
e. fortune

8 Which of these is wrong?
a. a maiden voyage
b. a maiden speech
c. a maiden name
d. a maiden servant
e. a maiden over

9 An American calls this man *a mortician*. An Englishman calls him
a. a forensic scientist
b. an undertaker
c. a bursar
d. a coroner
e. a sexton

10 Here are five seats: which of them is often higher or lower than the others?
- a. a bench
- b. a sofa
- c. a settee
- d. a settle
- e. a stool

11 Which phrase goes with the picture?
- a. a progress report
- b. reporting for duty
- c. a loud report
- d. the annual report
- e. an eye-witness report

12 Which of these can you do in silence?
- a. argue
- b. discuss
- c. dispute
- d. disagree
- e. contradict

13 Ashtrays, waste paper bins and dustbins are all
- a. containers
- b. holders
- c. receivers
- d. receptacles
- e. vessels

14 One sign of surprise is the . . . of the eyebrows.
a. heightening
b. elevating
c. rearing
d. exalting
e. raising

15 Finish this proverb: A . . . broom sweeps clean.
a. new
b. modern
c. fresh
d. up-to-date
e. novel

16 Instead of saying, *I'm sorry for being late*, you could say, *I . . . for being late*.
a. confess
b. repent
c. regret
d. apologise
e. admit

17 The words *polling, ballot* and *candidate* all have something to do with
a. sport
b. interviews
c. examinations
d. elections
e. the theatre

18 Twenty-one and twenty-two are
a. adjacent numbers
b. near numbers
c. neighbouring numbers
d. handy numbers
e. intimate numbers

19 Which phrase goes with the picture?
- a. holding forth
- b. holding the baby
- c. hold your tongue
- d. a hold-up
- e. a hold-all

20 Which of these do you do when you are sad?
- a. complain
- b. grumble
- c. lament
- d. grouse
- e. make a fuss

Unit nine

1 What is a masterstroke?
- a. a man patting his dog's head
- b. a punishment for a schoolboy
- c. the sound of Big Ben
- d. a very skilful act
- e. a heart attack

2 Finish this phrase: as pleased as
a. Paul
b. Pan
c. Punch
d. Peter
e. Judy

3 We call someone a minor because he is
a. inferior
b. smaller
c. under age
d. second-rate
e. unimportant

4 If you are talking shop, you are
a. chatting to a friend in a shop
b. discussing your purchases
c. stock-taking
d. talking about your work
e. trying to persuade a customer to buy something

5 The words *patient*, *ward* and *theatre* all have something to do with
a. hospitals
b. card games
c. plays
d. elections
e. doctors

6 Here are the names of five flowers: which one is also a colour?
a. lilac
b. gladioli
c. dahlia
d. freesia
e. salvia

7 Which goes with the picture?
a. a slide rule
b. having a slide
c. a slide projector
d. a hair slide
e. a landslide

☐

8 Which could be friendly?
a. a slap on the back
b. a thump on the back
c. a punch on the back
d. a poke in the back
e. a blow on the back

☐

9 Which of these is nearest in meaning to *an excursion*?
a. a trip
b. a journey
c. a voyage
d. an expedition
e. a tour

☐

10 If a man is kept in prison before his trial, he is held in
a. safety
b. security
c. preservation
d. protection
e. custody

☐

11 We keep valuables under . . . and key.
a. lock
b. padlock
c. bolt
d. chain
e. bar

☐

12 Finish this proverb: You can lead a horse to water, but you can't make him

a. drink
b. sip
c. imbibe
d. swallow
e. quaff

13 An American says *an elevator* when an Englishman says

a. a moving staircase
b. a lift
c. a hoist
d. an escalator
e. a conveyor belt

14 The sharp points on running shoes are

a. thorns
b. spikes
c. barbs
d. spines
e. horns

15 All these words mean *not bending easily*, but which one describes a thick piece of paper?

a. stiff
b. rigid
c. tense
d. inflexible
e. unbending

16 All these can mean *frightened*. Which is the strongest?

a. horrified
b. scared
c. startled
d. alarmed
e. petrified

17 What's the doctor saying?
a. There's something in the wind.
b. I've got my second wind.
c. Don't get the wind up.
d. You've taken the wind out of my sails.
e. You're sound in wind and limb.

18 Complete this phrase: for . . . years.
a. horse's
b. donkey's
c. ass's
d. mare's
e. pony's

19 Someone who works for his country's enemies is guilty of
a. disloyalty
b. infidelity
c. treachery
d. falseness
e. treason

20 Which word cannot complete this sentence? *Don't talk*
a. nonsense
b. rubbish
c. absurdity
d. gibberish
e. drivel

Unit ten

1 What does a doctor carry with him?
a. apparatus
b. appliances
c. instruments
d. gear
e. tackle

2 *Correct* is to *incorrect* as *legible* is to
a. illegible
b. inlegible
c. unlegible
d. dislegible
e. delegible

3 If you get a tiny piece of wood in your finger, what do you call it?
a. a splint
b. a sliver
c. a fragment
d. a slice
e. a splinter

4 The *source* can mean the *beginning* or *origin*, but which of these is wrong?
a. the source of a journey
b. the source of a river
c. the source of inspiration
d. the source of supply
e. the source of information

5 If you collect cuttings from newspapers and magazines, where do you usually keep them?
a. in a diary
b. in an album
c. in a catalogue
d. in a scrapbook
e. in a register

6 Which phrase goes with the picture?
a. a fire extinguisher
b. a firelighter
c. a fire fighter
d. a firebrand
e. a fireplace

7 Finish this proverb: All work and no play makes . . . a dull boy.
a. Harry
b. Dick
c. Jack
d. Tom
e. John

8 Which of these lasts for a very short time?
a. a glow
b. a flash
c. a gleam
d. a flame
e. a blaze

9 When people get married, they are . . . in matrimony.
a. fixed
b. joined
c. attached
d. secured
e. fastened

10 Which man did not speak?
a. He duplicated my words.
b. He repeated my words.
c. He imitated my words.
d. He echoed my words.
e. He reiterated my words.

11 An American says *a cookie* when an Englishman would say
a. a cake
b. a biscuit
c. a crisp
d. a sweet
e. a toffee

12 Which of these is not a block?
a. a heavy wooden butcher's table
b. a number of buildings joined together
c. a large piece of meat
d. a group of seats in a theatre
e. the main part of a petrol engine

13 Instead of *just in time*, we can say *in the . . . of time*.
a. second
b. split
c. notch
d. nick
e. point

14 Lines on the face are called

a. pleats
b. folds
c. overlaps
d. creases
e. wrinkles

15 If clothes get smaller when you wash them, they

a. contract
b. shrink
c. lessen
d. decrease
e. diminish

16 A man asked five girls to marry him. Which one said no most kindly?

a. She refused him.
b. She declined his offer.
c. She rejected him.
d. She rebuffed him.
e. She repulsed his offer.

17 Which phrase goes with the picture?

a. a stroke of luck
b. sunstroke
c. the stroke of a pen
d. on the stroke
e. breaststroke

18 If someone gives you the cold shoulder, he
a. gives you a piece of meat to eat
b. pats you on the back
c. tackles you in a football game
d. speaks frankly and openly to you
e. refuses to speak to you

19 If you call someone a bloke, what does it mean?
a. You think he is stupid.
b. You are using informal language.
c. You like him.
d. You dislike him.
e. He is a member of your family.

20 Which word would be wrong? *The water . . . from the tap.*
a. oozed
b. poured
c. gushed
d. spouted
e. trickled

Unit eleven

1 When you put plants in a garden, you
a. station them
b. lodge them
c. situate them
d. locate them
e. set them

2 Which word describes a person who gives to the poor?
a. charitable
b. generous
c. liberal
d. hospitable
e. open-handed

3 Which does not have a crown?
a. a house
b. a road
c. a hill
d. a head
e. a tooth

4 Which of these has something to do with the aristocracy?
a. once in a blue moon
b. a bolt from the blue
c. to scream blue murder
d. blue blood in his veins
e. a blue film

5 If you put your cards on the table, you
a. resign from your job
b. state your intentions openly
c. cheat at cards
d. hand in your notice
e. send out party invitations

6 A stop-watch is
a. a broken watch
b. a guard
c. a sideshow
d. the television on/off switch
e. a special watch used in timing a race

7 In Britain, Christmas holidays are an old

a. habit
b. practice
c. tradition
d. usage
e. routine

8 Which means *the car went backwards*?

a. it reared
b. it backfired
c. it returned
d. it went
e. it reversed

9 The words *lens*, *shutter* and *to load* all have something to do with

a. cameras
b. ships
c. the eye
d. windows
e. trains

10 One English king was called Richard the Lion-heart. Why was this?

a. He had yellow hair.
b. He was brave.
c. He had a large heart.
d. He had a big chest.
e. He wore the picture of a lion on his chest.

11 Which of these flowers grows taller than a man?

a. a hollyhock
b. a hyacinth
c. a lupin
d. a pansy
e. a poppy

12 How do you make scissors sharp?
- a. you pare them
- b. you grind them
- c. you shave them
- d. you file them
- e. you scrape them

13 Which word describes a light-hearted and cheerful person?
- a. light
- b. weightless
- c. flimsy
- d. trivial
- e. buoyant

14 This sailor is carrying
- a. a kitbag
- b. a rucksack
- c. a haversack
- d. a satchel
- e. a carrier

15 If an English train arrives at Platform 2, an American train arrives at
- a. Band 2
- b. Lane 2
- c. Line 2
- d. Station 2
- e. Track 2

16 Which of these is right?
- a. a fake limb
- b. an artificial limb
- c. a dummy limb
- d. a simulated limb
- e. a mock limb

17 Finish this proverb: Money is the . . . of all evil.

a. foundation
b. foot
c. base
d. root
e. bottom

18 To reassure a friend you might say: *I'll stand by you through thick and*

a. thin
b. thicket
c. solid
d. spindly
e. murky

19 What are they doing?

a. serving time
b. keeping time
c. passing the time
d. passing the time of day
e. playing for time

20 Which of these is wrong?

a. a pleasant smell
b. a pleasant odour
c. a pleasant stench
d. a pleasant scent
e. a pleasant aroma

Unit twelve

1 All these words mean *to go round,* but what do the hands of a clock do?
a. roll
b. revolve
c. spin
d. rotate
e. circulate

2 Which of these has a different meaning from the others?
a. He pretended he was dead.
b. He feigned death.
c. He shammed death.
d. He imagined he was dead.
e. He simulated death.

3 An American says *cotton* when an Englishman says
a. thread
b. cotton wool
c. string
d. twine
e. wool

4 Which of these is wrong?
a. a dash of milk
b. to cut a dash
c. a dashboard
d. a dash for shelter
e. a dash of anger

5 The open end of a gun is called its
a. muzzle
b. mouth
c. opening
d. throat
e. orifice

6 If you show someone a clean pair of heels, what does it mean?
a. You run away from him as fast as you can.
b. You show him a pair of shoes you have just cleaned.
c. You have just washed your feet.
d. You turn your back on him.
e. You have holes in your socks.

7 Which word cannot describe someone who is old?
a. aged
b. antique
c. venerable
d. senile
e. elderly

8 Finish this proverb: He who laughs last laughs
a. many a long day
b. ever so long
c. for a long time
d. all the day long
e. longest

9 What do we call a bundle of corn?
a. a sheath
b. a sheaf
c. a stack
d. a bunch
e. a clump

10 Which phrase goes with the picture?
a. a passing out parade
b. making a pass
c. pass along, please
d. holding the pass
e. give the password

11 When you buy something and don't mind how much you spend, you buy it . . . the cost.
a. inattentive to
b. ignorant of
c. regardless of
d. insensible of
e. unconscious of

12 If someone says to you, *You're chicken*, what does he mean?
a. You make a lot of noise.
b. You brood over things.
c. You are sitting on a nest-egg.
d. You are a coward.
e. You are easily ruffled.

13 Which pain is the strongest?
a. a twinge
b. an ache
c. stinging
d. agony
e. smarting

14 Which one of these means *to show courage*?
a. to put on a bold face
b. to keep a straight face
c. to pull a long face
d. to lose face
e. to have a face-lift

☐

15 The words *Cabinet, constituency* and *Whip* all have something to do with
a. politics
b. riding
c. woodwork
d. cooking
e. furniture

☐

16 Which of these means a member of a group which moves about with no fixed home?
a. a pilgrim
b. a nomad
c. a vagrant
d. an adventurer
e. a tourist

☐

17 A weapon that can kill is a . . . one.
a. mortal
b. fatal
c. homicidal
d. killing
e. lethal

☐

18 Which would you not expect to find in a factory or an office?
a. a manager
b. an administrator
c. a sovereign
d. a director
e. a supervisor

☐

19 Which of these is wrong?
a. a beam of light
b. a baked beam
c. a beam of delight
d. a beam across a ceiling
e. broad in the beam

20 What is this game?
a. kisses and rings
b. crosses and circles
c. right and wrong
d. O's and X's
e. noughts and crosses

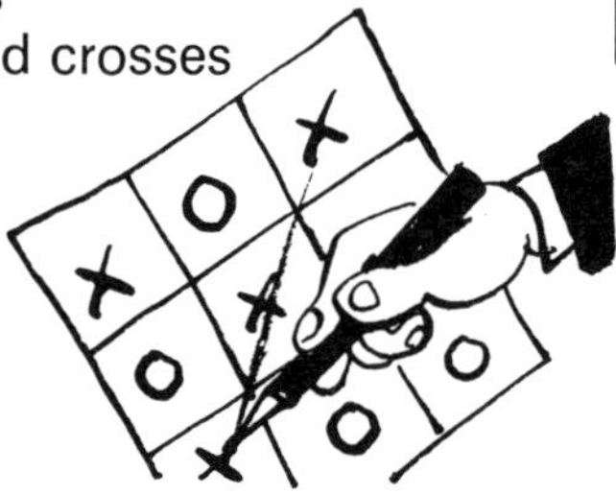

Unit thirteen

1 Which word does not mean *without end*?
a. pointless
b. ceaseless
c. interminable
d. perpetual
e. incessant

2 Finish this proverb: . . . the pennies and the pounds will . . . themselves.
a. Look through
b. Look at
c. Look up
d. Look after
e. Look for

3 If you get hold of the wrong end of the stick, you
a. are clumsy
b. get a splinter of wood in your finger
c. are poor at hockey
d. misunderstand something
e. play the violin badly

4 The words *key*, *scale* and *contour* all have something to do with
a. music
b. fish
c. maps
d. doors
e. weight

5 An American says *candy* when an Englishman says
a. syrup
b. sweets
c. sugar
d. cakes
e. biscuits

6 What do we call the bottom part of the ear?
a. an ear lobe
b. an earring
c. an ear drop
d. an earache
e. an earphone

7 A medicine ball is
- a. a pill
- b. a dance for nurses
- c. a large, heavy ball used for keeping fit
- d. a way of dancing to cure sick people
- e. a drop of medicine

☐

8 Which of these means *to throw up into the air*?
- a. to hurl
- b. to project
- c. to toss
- d. to heave
- e. to propel

☐

9 He is . . . the cards
- a. distributing
- b. dispensing
- c. dealing
- d. assigning
- e. allotting

☐

10 Which of these has the meaning of *something wrong*?
- a. an occurrence
- b. a disaster
- c. an incident
- d. a happening
- e. an event

☐

11 Which kind of fear is strongest?
a. timidity
b. fright
c. anxiety
d. panic
e. concern

12 The flag of the USSR shows the hammer and
a. scythe
b. spade
c sickle
d. shears
e. blade

13 To keep a dog in England you must have
a. a charter
b. permission
c. a permit
d. a licence
e. a sanction

14 When you put a coin in a machine, you
a. intrude it
b. insinuate it
c. inject it
d. infiltrate it
e. insert it

15 A German student said, *I haven't had the possibility of seeing the film*. He should have said, *I haven't had the*
a. probability
b. opportunity
c. feasibility
d. practicability
e. potential

16 A well-known nursery rhyme starts: Hey diddle diddle,
- a. My name is Tom Tiddle
- b. I'll tell you a riddle
- c. The grid and the griddle
- d. The cat and the fiddle
- e. The pig in the middle

17 Which phrase goes with the picture?
- a. in the balance
- b. a balance wheel
- c. the balance of power
- d. strike a balance
- e. keeping his balance

18 Which of these is an unwanted possession?
- a. the white of an egg
- b. a white elephant
- c. white horses
- d. a white feather
- e. a white lie

19 If you tell a lie in a court of law, you commit
a. perjury
b. an untruth
c. a falsehood
d. a forgery
e. a fib

20 *Lax* can mean *not firm*. Which of these can be lax?
a. a piece of string
b. pronunciation
c a collar
d. discipline
e. a seat

Unit fourteen

1 Which of these is wrong?
a. an orchestral conductor
b. a water conductor
c. a lightning conductor
d. a bus conductor
e. an electrical conductor

2 The words *rafter, eaves* and *lintel* all have something to do with
a. boat building
b. plants
c. house building
d. the sea
e. first aid

3 If you are in the red, what does it mean?
a. You are feeling embarrassed.
b. You are a communist.
c. You have scarlet fever.
d. Your bank account is overdrawn.
e. You have been caught doing something wrong.

4 Which of these do we not say?
a. a public army
b. a public school
c. public conveniences
d. a public library
e. a public house

5 *A thumb tack* is the American word for
a. a nail
b. a drawing pin
c. a screw
d. a rivet
e. a pin

6 Finish this phrase: as thin as
a. a rake
b. a harrow
c. a trowel
d. a fork
e. a hoe

7 Which of these does a house not have?
a. a door
b. a gateway
c. an entrance
d. an inlet
e. a threshold

8 What is she using?
a. a pump
b. a press
c. an air gun
d. a syringe
e. a blower

9 Which of these is wrong?
a. an antique car
b. an old car
c. a veteran car
d. an antiquated car
e. a vintage car

10 All of these mean *miserable* but only one can describe the weather.
a. dismal
b. sorrowful
c. melancholy
d. unhappy
e. sad

11 Finish this proverb: Time and tide wait for no
a. chap
b. fellow
c. gentleman
d. person
e. man

12 A child whose parents are not married is

a. unlawful
b. illegal
c. illegitimate
d. prohibited
e. unauthorised

13 Complete this phrase: by hook or by

a. crook
b. nail
c. book
d. handle
e. eye

14 What sound does a cow make?

a. it coos
b. it lows
c. it hoots
d. it drones
e. it roars

15 Which of these is least strong?

a. to hate
b. to detest
c. to abhor
d. to dislike
e. to loathe

16 When a football team wins a game, they

a. beat the other team
b. conquer the other team
c. overcome the other team
d. vanquish the other team
e. overthrow the other team

17 Which phrase goes with the picture?
a. press on
b. press-ups
c. time presses
d. the press box
e. press studs

18 A sudden surprise is a bolt out of the
a. blue
b. red
c. green
d. yellow
e. black

19 If you are in front of all the other runners in a race, you are
a. the forerunner
b. the header
c. the precedent
d. the prefix
e. the leader

20 The words *queen*, *hive* and *cell* all have something to do with
a. batteries
b. royalty
c. chess
d. bees
e. prison

Unit fifteen

1 Who went up the hill to fetch a pail of water?
a. Wendy and Will
b. George and Lill
c. Tom and Bill
d. Pete and Phil
e. Jack and Jill

2 Which of these are least satisfactory?
a. moderate results
b. average results
c. fair results
d. mediocre results
e. modest results

3 All these are the names of different kinds of boats. Which one carries passengers?
a. a tanker
b. a liner
c. a coaster
d. a freighter
e. a trawler

4 If someone offering you a chair says, *Take a pew*, he is being
a. rude
b. very serious
c. mildly amusing
d. unfriendly
e. too friendly

5 Which of these has a hilt?
a. a knife
b. a razor
c. a sword
d. scissors
e. a saw

6 Which of these is female?
a. a gander
b. a filly
c. a drake
d. a stallion
e. a ram

7 The words *second*, *ring* and *Break!* all have something to do with
a. clocks
b. boxing
c. marriage
d. weather
e. time

8 These are all kinds of punishment. Which of them means you must pay money?
a. a fine
b. a penalty
c. a penance
d. a forfeit
e. confiscation

9 If you are telling someone to be careful, you say, *Don't run any*
a. risks
b. dangers
c. perils
d. threats
e. jeopardy

10 An American says *a trash can* when an Englishman says
a. a waste-paper basket
b. a rubbish tip
c. a refuse can
d. a litter basket
e. a dustbin

☐

11 Finish this proverb: A . . . and his money are soon parted.
a. fool
b. half-wit
c. blockhead
d. idiot
e. simpleton

☐

12 Which phrase goes with the picture?
a. pulling him round
b. pulling him to pieces
c. pulling his socks up
d. pulling his weight
e. pulling faces

☐

13 When you enter for an examination, you are

a. a competitor
b. an applicant
c. a candidate
d. a claimant
e an opponent

14 Which of these is wrong?

a. a tight shoe
b. a tight corridor
c. a tight string
d. a tight corner
e. tight-fisted

15 A book which deals with subjects which are interesting at the present time is

a. modern
b. up-to-date
c. topical
d. novel
e. fashionable

16 Which of these is not a catch?

a. a sudden sight of something
b. a trick
c. what a fisherman has caught
d. something for fastening a door
e. the action of catching a ball

17 When you fight with all your strength, you fight tooth and
a. hands
b. fist
c nail
d. knuckle
e. feet

18 Which phrase goes with the picture?
a. pole-vaulting
b. poles apart
c. up the pole
d. the pole star
e. the magnetic pole

19 Which of these is not a member of a profession?
a. a doctor
b. a dentist
c. a teacher
d. a bus driver
e. an actor

20 If you cut a piece of paper with a pair of scissors, you
a. saw it
b. chop it
c. carve it
d. snip it
e. slash it

Answers

Unit one

1 **b.** All these people judge something. *An examiner* judges the quality of work, of a product, or an examination. *An adjudicator* judges a contest or competition. *A judge* = (legal) the chief figure in a court of law, but also has a general sense (I am a poor judge of character). Sports like boxing, football, rugby, have *a referee*.

2 **e.** *Molten* = melted by heat (molten lead, iron). *Sultry* and *close* = very warm, humid and oppressive (as before a thunderstorm). *Sweltering* and *torrid* = very, very hot.

3 **b.** *With bated breath* = (a fixed phrase) tense, excited. *Bated* is only used in this phrase.

4 **c.** *Permanent* = remaining, staying the same for a long time (a permanent wave makes hair stay curly for a long time). *Everlasting* = (literally) lasting for ever (an everlasting discussion would be tiresomely long). *Habitual* = usual, happening regularly (habitual drinking). *Established* = fixed, decided (an established fact, an established rule). *Persistent* = repeated, continuing (persistent questions, a persistent illness).

5 **e.** *A sheath* = the cover for the blade of a weapon (a sword, a dagger). *A wallet* = a small, flat case for holding banknotes which fits into a pocket.

6 **c.** (A fixed phrase.) *A sinew* = a strong cord joining the muscle to the bone. *Gristle* is found in meat and is rubbery and difficult to chew.

7 **b.** *Legal* = to do with the law (the legal profession, legal action). *Lawful* = allowed by the law, according to law (his lawful wife). *Legitimate* = rightful (legitimate demands, legitimate children). *Authorised* = fixed by authority (the authorised version of the Bible, an authorised statement). *Legalised* = made legal (legalised theft).

8 **c.** *To keep your head* = (colloquial) to stay calm. *To keep your head above water* = to avoid getting into debt. *To keep up appearances* = to put on an outward show, hiding the true state of affairs (e.g. running a large car when you cannot afford it). *To keep up with the Joneses* = to copy and compete with your neighbour (especially his possessions).

9 **d.** We also *construct* an argument, a plan, a theory. *Making* and *producing* are general words (cars are made or produced in factories; cows make or produce milk). *Manufacturing* = making things in large quantities by machine. We *compose* a letter, a poem, a tune.

10 **c.** *To trudge* = to walk with heavy steps. *To stride* = to walk in a purposeful way, taking long paces. *To strut* and *to stalk* = to walk along stiffly and haughtily. *To amble* = to walk slowly and aimlessly.

11 **a.** (Colloquial.) *Washroom* is more usual in America than in Britain.

12 **e**

13 **d.** *Audacious* = bold (from the Latin 'audere', to dare; the others come from 'audire', to hear). *An audition* = a test performance by an entertainer to show his ability. *Audible* = able to be heard. *An auditorium* = the hall in which *an audience* sits.

14 **b.** *A discussion* is usually friendly. In *an argument* or *dispute* people disagree. *A*

controversy = a matter about which people have differing opinions (especially social and political matters). *A contradiction* = a denial of what someone has said (I must contradict that statement of yours).

15 **e.** (A fixed phrase.) *Plumage* = feathers when they are still on the bird. *A plume* = a large, soft feather (for decoration on a hat). *A quill* = a large, stiff feather (once used for writing). *Down* = the soft feathers of a young bird (used in quilts and eiderdowns).

16 **a.** *A transept* = the part of *a church* which crosses the main building at right angles (symbolising the shorter arms of the cross). *An altar* = the table where the cross stands, the central point around which a service is conducted. *A pew* = a wooden bench seat for members of the congregation.

17 **c.** You might feel *elated* on receiving good news, or on passing an examination. *Genial* = friendly and *cheerful*. *Sprightly* = lively. *Blithe* = (poetic) gay.

18 **c.** The proverb means that we should not behave badly ourselves, just because someone else treats us badly.

19 **b.** *A bull's-eye* = a hit in the centre of the target. *A bull in a china shop* = a clumsy person (who breaks things). *A bullring* = the arena where bullfights are held. *A bulldog* = a large, powerful breed of dog.

20 **b.** *A piece of music* may call up *images* in your mind as you listen. The others are all different meanings of image. *An idol* = a carved figure worshipped as a god.

Unit two

1 **b.** The first line of the nursery rhyme goes:

Old King Cole was a merry old soul.

2 **e.** We say: I'll be with you *in a twinkling*. In the twinkling of an eye = in an instant. *In a tick* = (colloquial) in a minute.
3 **a.** A fixed phrase.
4 **a.** *To hold your breath* = to stop breathing for a few moments (from fear, excitement, or to keep quiet). *To peg out* is slang. *To breathe your last* and *to end your days* are more literary expressions. *To pass away* is the sort of expression used in a newspaper announcement of a death, or on a tombstone.
5 **c.** 'A chair', 'an idea', 'anger' are all *nouns*. 'The boy' is the *subject* of this sentence: The boy caught the ball. Notice: if your nationality is Swedish, you are a Swedish subject. 'No', 'not' and 'neither' are *negatives*; also, in photography, a negative is a plate with light and dark shades reversed.
6 **d.** This is offensive when it is said seriously.
7 **c.** *To play gooseberry* = to be present with two lovers who would prefer to be alone. *Goose-flesh* = skin covered in tiny bumps from cold or fear. *A gooseberry fool* = a dessert made from stewed gooseberries, cream and sugar. *A goose-step* = a way of marching without bending the legs. *A wild goose chase* = an unsuccessful and pointless search or journey.
8 **d.** *Refined* = purified (but we talk about purified *water*, not refined **water**).
9 **a.** *To give an order* in a restaurant = to tell the waiter what you want to eat. The others mean to tell someone what to do. *To command* and *to dictate* are strong words (military and political leaders may command or dictate).
10 **a.** A *brief* or *concise* answer uses few words but is not impolite. *Abbreviated* = shortened (Feb. is an abbreviation for February).

11 **d.** The proverb means that caution is better than courage: there is no point in taking unnecessary risks.

12 **b.** *A flyover* = a road which crosses over the top of another (usually on a motorway). *A viaduct* = a long bridge which carries a road across a valley. *A junction* = a place where several roads or railway lines meet.

13 **c.** A fixed phrase.

14 **d.** *A competitor* = someone who takes part in a race or a contest. *A claimant* = someone who makes a claim (a claim for damages or compensation in a law court, or a claim to a title or a throne). *An opponent* = someone you fight (a boxer, a person who disagrees with you), or play against (in chess, bridge, etc). *A rival* = someone who is competing with you for the same thing (a prize, a job). Companies who manufacture the same goods are rivals.

15 **d.** *A shoe* may well do all the other things but we usually say that it *pinches*. The other verbs usually have an object (This shoe squashes my toes).

16 **d.** *A demonstration* = a public display of feeling (usually over a political or social question: demonstrators march, carry banners, listen to speeches, and are not normally violent). *A mutiny* = a rebellion by a ship's crew against the captain. *A revolution* = a rebellion against the established order (of government, society, education, etc). *A riot* = a sudden, violent fight involving many people. *An insurrection* = an uprising (usually against the government).

17 **b.** *A foster child* = a child temporarily placed in the care of a person who acts as *a parent* (a foster mother or father), but is not a legal *guardian*.

18 **b.** *Rays* = beams of light (especially from the sun). *Radii* = lines from the centre of a circle to its circumference. *A joiner* = a carpenter who makes the woodwork inside buildings.

19 **b.** *To put your foot down* = to be very firm. *To put in an appearance* = to pay a very short visit somewhere (possibly out of a sense of duty). *To put two and two together* = to consider the facts and arrive at a conclusion. *To put your foot in it* = to make a blunder. *To put someone off his stroke* = to interrupt what someone is doing, making him hesitate.

20 **a.** The correct sentence is: *Your life is threatened.*

Unit three

1 **b.** *Highbrow* is often used contemptuously to mean intellectual (highbrow music, highbrow people). Notice: a brow = *a forehead*; also, *the top of a hill. The line of hair above the eye* = the eyebrow.

2 **d.** *Kin* is an old word for relatives and is rarely used except in this phrase. We never say the others.

3 **e.** *On the rocks* = poured over ice cubes. Drinks like whisky and gin which are served in small quantities are called shorts, as opposed to long drinks like beer and lager.

4 **d.** *To depart* = to leave. *To flee* = (literary) to escape. When a person *absconds*, it is usually because he has done something wrong (to abscond from prison). *To retreat* = to move back to a safer position (to retreat from the enemy).

5 **e.** All the others are metaphorical ways of saying: I am extremely angry. Water *boils* when heated to a temperature of 100°C. *To fume* = to give off smoke or gas. *To simmer* = to keep at boiling point. *To blaze* = to burn brightly.

6 **c.** *A hat trick* = (cricket) taking three wickets with three consecutive balls; or three consecutive goals in football. *A brim* = the lower edge which juts out on a hat. *A turn-up* = the band of material which is folded upward at the bottom of a trouser leg. *A lapel* = part of a coat or jacket which is folded back and which is a continuation of the collar. *A vent* = a slit in the back of a jacket.

7 **d.** *A cartoon* = a lively, humorous line drawing. *An engraver* cuts out designs on hard surfaces like wood, metal or stone. *A caricature* = a humorous drawing of a person (exaggerated to make him appear ridiculous).

8 **c.** If you take news or information *with a pinch of salt*, you don't take it seriously.

9 **b.** *A comrade* is often used for a fellow member of a trade union or political party (especially the Communist party). *Pal, chum* (old-fashioned) and *buddy* (US) are very informal. *An ally* = someone who supports you in a dispute (often a country which supports another in a war).

10 **d.** *Hymns* are sung in church and *carols* are sung at Christmas time. *A chant* = monotonous, repetitive singing, similar to recitation (parts of a church service may be chanted). *A dirge* = a mournful song or hymn suitable for funerals.

11 **e.** *A tenant* pays money to live in a house which is owned by someone else. *An occupant* = the person who occupies or lives in a house, whether tenant or owner. *A proprietor* = *an owner* (of a shop, hotel, buildings).

12 **c.** *Deranged* can only describe a person.

13 **a.** The proverb means that as people get older it becomes harder for them to learn new things. Notice: people are *elderly* or *aged*; things are *antique* or *ancient*.

14 **b.** *To lay to rest* = to bury. *A hundred to one the rest* is an expression from betting: having given the odds on likely winners, a bookmaker may say *a hundred to one the rest*. That is, all the others have odds of a hundred to one against them winning. *Rest assured* (a fixed phrase) = Be sure, confident (Rest assured I shan't forget you). *To rest on your oars* = (an expression from rowing) to have a rest after exertion. *To rest on your laurels* = to rest because you are content with past successes.

15 **a.** All the other words = to pierce or to make a hole, but they apply to things, not people. You *puncture* a car tyre; *perforate* a piece of paper; *drill* or *bore* a hole in a hard surface. Notice: to bore = to make someone bored.

16 **b.** *Provisional*, *impermanent* and *transient* = lasting a short time, but they are wrong in this sentence. We talk about a provisional arrangement, a provisional driving licence; happiness may be impermanent or transient. *Extemporary* = done on the spur of the moment, with no preparation.

17 **c.** (A fixed phrase.) We do not use the other words in this phrase.

18 **a.** *The weapon carried by British policemen* = a truncheon (a short, thick stick).

19 **e.** *To take the lead* = to go into first position, ahead of the others. *To lead someone a dance* = to give someone trouble and waste his time by leading him from place to place. *To lead someone by the nose* = to make someone do whatever you want. *A juvenile lead* = a young actor playing a leading role. *To lead a double life* = to have interests and pursuits which you keep secret from your family and friends (a spy would probably have to lead a double life).

20 **a.** *A junction* = a point where roads or railway lines meet. *Points* = rails which move to allow trains to change tracks. *A cutting* = a place where the earth is cut away to make room for the railway track.

Unit four

1 **a.** The *shin* = the front of the leg below the knee. The *calf* = the back of the leg below the knee. The *thigh* = the leg above the knee.

2 **b.** *Dormant* = (not used for people) inactive at the present time (especially volcanoes).

3 **d.** If a child goes to a private *school*, its parents pay school fees. All the others are different meanings of *charge*.

4 **d.** *A violent man* might physically attack you. *Robust* = strong and healthy. *Energetic* = active. *Forceful* = strong and determined. *Vigorous* = forceful and energetic.

5 **b.** *Fragile* = delicate, easily broken (glassware, china). *Feeble* = weak (a feeble person, excuse, answer). *Impotent* = powerless. *Frail* = fragile (a frail old lady, a frail shelf).

6 **b.** *To burn the midnight oil* = to work late into the night. *Oilskins* = waterproof clothes (as worn by seamen over their ordinary clothes). *A study in oils* = a painting done with oil paints. *To pour oil on troubled waters* = to act as peacemaker when others are quarrelling. *To oil* (or grease) *someone's palm* = to bribe him.

7 **d**

8 **e.** *Cloak and dagger* = (a fixed phrase) to do with mystery and intrigue (a cloak and dagger existence, operation). *A doublet* = a tight-fitting jacket that men wore in the 17th century. *Breeches* = old-fashioned trousers which stop just below the knee.

9 **e.** *To pass a law* = to bring a new law into force. All the others mean *to break the law*.

10 **d.** *To jangle* = to make a harsh clanging noise (bells or a bunch of keys might jangle). *To chug* and *to throb* = to make a steady beating noise. *To splutter* = to cough, misfire. *To purr* = to make a low, continuous, agreeable sound.

11 **a.** *Stamps* have *perforated* edges to make them easy to tear off. *A watermark* = a distinguishing mark in paper which can be seen clearly by holding it up to the light (*banknotes* also have a watermark). *A sheet* of stamps = a page of stamps.

12 **c.** *Superfluous* = more than is needed, unwanted (superfluous hair on a woman's face). *Abundant* = plentiful (an abundant supply of apples). *Surplus* = more than is needed (to sell off surplus food at a low price). *Excessive* = too much (excessive pressure, excessive rudeness).

13 **e.** *A heading* = the word or words which appear at the top of a piece of writing, usually in larger print than the rest. *A nickname* = an affectionate or amusing name you give to someone instead of his real name. *A surname* = a family name (Smith, Jones). *A caption* = the words of explanation that appear with a picture in a book or newspaper.

14 **c.** The others have no meaning.

15 **b.** *Blaring* = the sound made by *a trumpet* or a car horn; also, a harsh, loud voice (usually a man's) can be blaring.

16 **a.** *To authorise* = (formal) to give official permission. *To sanction* = to give approval to something.

17 **b.** *To crow* and *to exult* = to rejoice at your own triumph, often at someone else's expense; also, crowing = the noise a cockerel makes.

18 **b.** *To pluck up courage* = (a fixed phrase) to find courage, to overcome your fears. *To pluck* = to pick or pull. *To jerk* and *to snatch* = to pull towards you with a sudden movement.

19 **e.** *A train* = a long robe which rests on the floor behind the wearer and which therefore needs to be carried. *A down train* = a train coming from the central terminus. *A trainee* = a person who is receiving training (for a job). Sportsmen are *in training* before a contest: they carry out a strict routine of exercises to make sure that they will be at the peak of their form. *A train of thought* = a sequence of thoughts (You have interrupted my train of thought.)

20 **c.** *A van* = a vehicle with an enclosed rear part for carrying goods. *A wagon* = an open truck for carrying goods on the railway. *A trailer* = a container for carrying goods which is pulled along by a lorry or car.

Unit five

1 **b.** *A muffler* = a thick scarf for the neck. The others are different styles of hat. *A bowler* = a black hat with a stiff, rounded crown (worn by businessmen). *A trilby* = a soft felt hat. *A beret* = a flat, round, soft hat (worn by some schoolgirls and soldiers). *A deerstalker* = a close-fitting hat with flaps to cover the ears (worn by sportsmen when out hunting).

2 **a.** *A ventilator* = a device (e.g. a fan) which provides fresh air. The others are different types of passage. *A funnel* = a ship's chimney. *A shaft* = a vertical passage (a lift shaft, a mine shaft).

3 **a.** The correct phrase is: *broken pencils.* *Ruined children* have been spoilt by over-indulgent parents.

4 **d.** We *recoil* from anything frightening or horrible in fear or disgust; we *retreat* in fear, or weakness (a retreating army); flood waters *recede* as they dry up; a memory recedes or fades; we *withdraw* from a room when we leave it, or from a competition if we decide not to take part. *To rebound* = to bounce back.

5 **b.** The proverb means that we have little regard or respect for things or people that are very well known to us. *To generate* = *to produce* (to generate electricity, steam). *To beget* = to produce as a parent (to beget children). *To rear* = to take care of children and young animals.

6 **a.** *An occurrence* = a happening, an event. *A disorder* = a disturbance, especially of health (a stomach disorder, a mental disorder). *A crisis* = the peak of trouble, a turning-point (The country is in a state of crisis). *An emergency* = a serious *accident* or situation which requires swift action.

7 **a.** *A pebble* = a small, round *stone. A rock* = a large, unshaped stone. *A crag* = a high, rough mass of rock. *A cliff* = a steep rock face, often on the sea shore.

8 **c.** *An income* = all the money you receive (whether as a salary, an allowance, or from investments). *Winnings* = money gained from gambling, winning contests. *A salary* = the money you are paid for doing a job. *An acquisition* = something you have obtained (not necessarily money).

9 **a.** *A part of the circumference of a circle* = an arc. Notice: *bow* meaning part of a ship rhymes with cow. For the other meanings it rhymes with throw.

10 **b.** *To all intents and purposes* = (a fixed phrase) in all important respects.

11 **a.** *An alternative* and *an option* = something

that may be chosen (You have several alternatives, options to choose from). *A selection* = things that are chosen (Make your own selection).

12 **c.** The ten *commandments* are the laws given by God to Moses. We talk about the *laws* of a country, the *rules* of a society. *Regulations* = (formal) rules (traffic regulations, safety regulations). *An order* = an instruction.

13 **e.** You can *applaud* by clapping your hands. *To praise* and *to commend* = to speak favourably of someone. *To compliment* = to express admiration (often for a person's physical appearance). *To flatter* = to pay insincere compliments.

14 **b.** *A stepson* = the son by an earlier marriage of your present husband or wife. *Out of step* = (literally) not putting your foot down at the same time as the person you are walking with; (metaphorically) not in harmony with others. *Step by step* = gradually, steadily. *Stepping stones* = stones which provide a path above the surface of water or mud.

15 **b.** *Expensive* = costing a lot of money. *Affluent* and *monied* = (formal) *wealthy*. *Well-to-do* = (colloquial) wealthy.

16 **b.** In Britain, the *hood* of a car = the soft, folding roof of a sports car.

17 **b.** To have *second thoughts* = to change your mind after thinking carefully or *reflecting* on something. *Second sight* = the power to see into the future. *In arrears* = late, behindhand (with payments or work). *In retrospect* = looking back at something which happened in the past (to see a situation in retrospect).

18 **a.** The other words have similar meanings but are wrong here. *Gear* is a general word for equipment: hunting gear, sailing gear (the

clothes and instruments you need for these activities). *Tackle* = equipment for fishing. *Apparatus* = technical equipment (gymnastic, chemistry apparatus).

19 **a.** *To mark down* = to lower the price of something. *A birthmark* = a mark on the body at birth. *To mark time* = (literally) to march on the spot; (metaphorically) to wait until you can move on again. *To make your mark* = to become distinguished. *A marked man* = a man singled out by enemies to be watched or hunted.

20 **d.** Gooseberries are green: the others are black.

Unit six

1 **c.** *A beginner* = someone who is new to something (a course of study, a job). *A starter* = someone who gives the signal for a race to start; also, someone who competes in a race; also, (colloquial) the first course of a meal. *A primary* = a preliminary stage of an election in the USA. *A maiden* = (old-fashioned) a young woman. Notice: a maiden voyage = a ship's first voyage; a maiden speech = the first speech in Parliament by a new member.

2 **c.** The plural form of *gas* = *gases*.

3 **b.** *A fibre* = a thread-like material (many modern clothes are made of man-made fibres). *A stripe* = a band of colour (zebras have black and white stripes). *A strip* = a long, thin piece (a strip of cloth, paper).

4 **d.** *A guffaw* = a loud, hearty *laugh*. *Giggles, titters* and *chuckles* = quiet, suppressed laughter, giggles and titters being high-pitched, chuckles low-pitched.

5 **b.** Notice: to crop up = to occur suddenly, unexpectedly. The others are different meanings of *crop*.

6 **b.** All the other words mean the *top*. We talk about the *peak* of a hill, the peak of excitement,

the peak of success; the *summit* of a mountain, a summit conference; the *crown* of a person's head.

7 **d.** A fixed phrase.

8 **d.** *Out of your mind* and *out of your senses* = mad, deranged. *Out of your element* = ill at ease with your surroundings (perhaps among people you do not get on with). *Out of your class* = among people who are in some way greatly superior to you.

9 **e.** *A spinster* = an unmarried woman (usually an older woman). *A virgin* = a person (especially a woman) who has had no sexual intercourse. *A widow* = a woman whose husband is dead (a man whose wife is dead = a widower). *A damsel* = (old-fashioned) a young woman. *A single girl* = an unmarried young woman.

10 **e.** *A grimace* = an expression showing annoyance or discomfort. *A snigger* = a suppressed, sarcastic laugh. *A grin* = a wide smile. *A smirk* = an unpleasant, self-satisfied smile.

11 **c.** *A gulf* = a part of the sea nearly surrounded by land (the Gulf of Mexico). *A bay* = part of the sea within the curve of the coast (the Bay of Biscay). *An inlet* = a smaller part of the sea extending into the land. *A cove* = a small bay.

12 **a.** *A stole* = a long, loose scarf for indoors, worn round the shoulders. *A cummerbund* = a broad, decorative belt, often of silk (worn by men wearing dinner jackets). *A girdle* = a belt to hold clothes in place; also, a kind of corset. *A sash* = a decorative cloth belt.

13 **d.** *To moor* = to tie up a boat safely. We *lodge* people as guests, we lodge complaints. We *pitch* a tent when we put it up. We *deposit* money in a bank.

14 **c.** *A profile* = a side view of the face. *An*

outline = the outside shape (an outline map). *A silhouette* = a solid black shape showing the outline but no detail (a man's silhouette against the sky). *A contour* = an outline, usually of hills, mountains, etc. *A cross-section* = a cutting through something to show the details inside (a cross-section of the Earth's crust to show the different layers of rock).

15 **a.** *To classify* = to put into classes. *To order flowers* = to buy them in advance. *To arrange flowers* = to put them tastefully in a vase. *To group flowers* = to arrange them in groups. *To divide flowers* = to share them out.

16 **b.** *Languidly* = slowly, without energy. The others mean *slowly*.

17 **c.** *A locomotive* = a railway engine. *A tender* = a wagon pulled behind an engine to carry fuel. *A pullman* = a luxury railway carriage. *A guard's van* = the last part of the train in which the guard travels.

18 **d.** *Livestock* = farm animals, especially cattle, sheep and pigs. *In the stocks* = being punished in an old-fashioned way, the feet being locked in a wooden framework. *A laughing stock* = someone who everyone laughs at. *Stocks and shares* = certificates of money lent and borrowed on the Stock Exchange. *Stock-taking* = a check on the goods in stock that a shop has for sale.

19 **d.** The proverb means the first people to arrive have the first choice.

20 **d.** *To swell* = to get bigger (a swollen finger, river, door). *To inflate* = to blow up with air or gas (a balloon, a bicycle tyre). *To extend* = to make bigger or longer (to extend your house, your visit); also, to stretch out (to extend your arm); also, to offer (to extend sympathy). *To increase* = to get bigger (a family, speed, prices increase). *To grow* = to get bigger (children, flowers grow).

Unit seven

1 **c.** *To hurl = to throw* violently (to hurl stones, weapons, abuse). *To cast* = to throw, to let fall (to cast a fishing line, to cast a shadow). *To pitch* = to throw (to pitch a ball). *To toss* = to throw carelessly (to toss a coin).

2 **e.** *I am naive* = I am simple, unsophisticated. The others are protestations of innocence. *Innocent = guiltless. Harmless* = not dangerous. *Blame* is less strong than guilt.

3 **e.** *To cradle* = to hold something lovingly and carefully in your arms. *To support* = to hold from below, not necessarily protectively. *To sustain* = to support, to keep up (to sustain life, an argument). *To bear* a child = to have a baby. *To maintain* a child = to provide for a child (to maintain a child at a private school).

4 **a.** *To challenge* = to dare someone to do something (especially if he seems reluctant). All the other words = to request very earnestly.

5 **d.** *Immortal* = never dying. *Ceaseless* = never stopping. *Never-ending* = without end (a never-ending story). *Everlasting* = lasting for ever (everlasting flowers). *Undying* = eternal (undying gratitude, loyalty, but not people).

6 **b.** The *wings* = (here) the side of a theatre stage. *On the wing* = flying (of birds). *The east wing* = the eastern part of a building. *To take under your wing* = to protect. *A wing chair* = an easy-chair with high side pieces.

7 **a.** *A dent* = a hollow made by striking a hard surface (a dent in metal, wood). *A recess* = a place where the wall of a room goes in (Put the piano in the recess). *A cave* = a large, natural hollow in rock. *A dimple* = a small hollow in the skin (a dimple in a cheek).

8 **a.** *Without rhyme or reason* = (a fixed phrase) incomprehensible, without any reason.

9 **e.** Lions *roar*, donkeys *bray*, dogs *snarl* and *growl* when they are angry.

10 **b.** (Colloquial.) *A jumble sale* = a sale of unwanted, secondhand items, often for charity.

11 **b.** *To meditate* = to think long and deeply, often on religious subjects. *To consider* and *to ponder* = to think seriously. *To reflect* = to think again. *To dream* = to imagine things (usually while sleeping).

12 **e.** The proverb means a task is lighter when many people help. Notice: *toil* = (literary) work.

13 **d.** Only *virgin* is used of *soil*. *Green* = immature, inexperienced. *Mint* = newly made, in new condition (a mint coin, stamp).

14 **a.** All these are tools. *A spanner* turns nuts. *A vice* grips things firmly. *A chisel* cuts away (as in shaping stone). *A hammer* hits. *A screwdriver* turns screws.

15 **b.** The *tide* = the twice daily rise and fall of the sea. The *swell* = the gentle rising and falling of the open sea. *Plankton* = tiny plants and animals which float in the sea.

16 **a.** When a man asks a woman to marry him, he makes *a proposal of marriage* (a fixed phrase). The others are all offers or suggestions, but not of marriage. Companies make business *tenders*. Card players and people at auctions make *bids*. Businessmen make *propositions*.

17 **d.** *To turn the scales* at 70 kg = to weigh 70 kg. *A pair of scales* = a simple weighing machine. *A minor scale* = a kind of musical scale. *To draw something to scale* = to draw something smaller but in proportion (architects' plans are drawn to scale). *On a small scale* = reduced in size; in a restricted way (to carry out experiments on a small scale).

18 **b.** (A polite and rather sympathetic description.) The others are unlikely to be used for people: a *round* building, shape; a *circular* route; a *spherical* object, spacecraft; an *oval* dish, flower bed.

19 **c.** *As right as rain* = (a fixed phrase) fit and well.

20 **a.** *A sketch* = a rough or preliminary drawing. *A portrait* = a drawing or painting of a person. *A miniature* = a very small painting. *A cartoon* = an amusing drawing; also, a preliminary sketch for a painting (the Leonardo cartoon). *A study* = an artist's exercise in drawing or painting.

Unit eight

1 **e.** All these are kinds of horses but we do not say *a riding horse*. Horses which carry riders have different names according to their special purposes (a hunter, *a racehorse*). The general word for a horse which carries a rider is a mount. *A rocking horse* = a child's wooden horse on which he sits and rocks. *A clothes horse* = a wooden stand for drying washing. *A vaulting horse* = a piece of gymnastic apparatus for jumping over.

2 **d.** *Offspring* = children or young animals (His offspring are all blonde). Notice: a mainspring = the driving spring in a watch or clock.

3 **b.** *Feverishly* = excitedly, fitfully, as though suffering from a fever. *To speak heatedly, warmly, fervently* and *ardently* = to speak in a very emotional way.

4 **a.** *To repulse* = to push back (The army repulsed the enemy). *To retort* = to answer back (No, he retorted). *To rejoin* = (here) to reply, to retort. *To rescind* = to cancel (to rescind a law).

5 **e.** *A coat of paint* = (a fixed phrase) a layer of

paint. Notice: an undercoat (a first coat of paint), a top coat (a last coat of paint). We talk about *a layer* or *a stratum* of rock.

6 **a.** Colloquial.

7 **e.** (A fixed phrase.) He went in search of *fame and fortune*.

8 **d.** A serving girl = *a maidservant. Maiden* = original, first. So *a maiden voyage* = a ship's first voyage. *A maiden speech* = a Member of Parliament's first speech. *A maiden name* = a woman's surname before marriage. *A maiden over* = six balls in cricket from which no runs are scored (He bowled a maiden over).

9 **b.** *An undertaker* arranges funerals. *A forensic scientist* = a scientist who works for courts of law. *A bursar* = a financial officer in a college. *A coroner* = an official who looks into the causes of an unexplained death. *A sexton* = a gravedigger.

10 **e.** *A stool* = a simple backless seat for one person, sometimes lower than a chair, sometimes higher (e.g. a bar stool in a pub). *A bench* = a long wooden seat, with or without a back (a park bench). *A settee* = a long comfortable seat with back and arms. *A settle* = (old-fashioned) a long wooden seat with back and arms.

11 **c.** *A loud report* = a loud bang. *A progress report* = a statement of progress. *To report for duty* = to be present and ready for duty. *An annual report* = a yearly statement. *An eye-witness report* = a statement by someone who saw something happen.

12 **d.** *To disagree* = to take a different view. Disagreement can be shown by gestures like shaking the head, as well as by speech. All the others involve talking.

13 **d.** *A receptacle* = a container into which we put (often unwanted) things. Boxes and cans are

containers. *A holder* is rarely used alone, but notice: a pen holder, a gas holder etc. *A receiver* = part of a telephone or radio that receives the message; also, a person who receives stolen goods. *A vessel* = (here) a hollow receptacle for liquids (bowls, basins, buckets and tubs).

14 **e.** We *raise* our *eyebrows*. *To heighten* = to increase (tension, colour, anger). *To elevate* = (literary and formal) to raise (to elevate the mind, to elevate a man to the peerage). *To rear* = (here) to rise up (horses rear on their hind legs). *To exalt* = (formal) to raise in dignity or rank (an exalted person).

15 **a.** The proverb means that a person new to a job may make great changes.

16 **d.** The others are wrong. The correct form is: *I confess* (*repent, regret, admit*) *that I am late*. To repent is stronger and more literary.

17 **d.** We cast votes for *election candidates* at a *polling* station. *A ballot* = an election.

18 **a.** *Adjacent* = next to each other (adjacent houses, seats). *Neighbouring* = near to each other (neighbouring houses, villages). *Handy* = useful, near at hand (a handy tool; the shops are handy). *Intimate* = close, personal (intimate conversations, details).

19 **d.** *A hold-up* = (here) stopping someone by force to rob them. *To hold forth* = to speak in public, usually at length. To be left *holding the baby* = (colloquial, metaphorical) to be left with unwanted responsibility. *To hold your tongue* = (colloquial) to be quiet. *A hold-all* = a soft carrying bag.

20 **c.** We *lament* with grief or pain. We *complain* or *grumble* with dissatisfaction. *To grouse*

= (colloquial) to grumble. *To make a fuss* = (colloquial) to make noisy complaints.

Unit nine

1 **d**

2 **c.** *As pleased as Punch* = (a fixed phrase) very pleased.

3 **c.** *A minor* = (here) a person under the legal age, usually eighteen.

4 **d**

5 **a.** *A patient* = a sick person having *hospital* treatment. Notice: in-patients stay in hospital, out-patients visit the hospital for treatment. *A ward* = a hospital room where patients live (a children's ward, an accident ward). *A theatre* = a room in a hospital where operations are performed; also, a building where plays are performed.

6 **a.** *Lilac* = also, the colour of the flower, a pale purple.

7 **b.** *A slide* = (here) a ride down a slippery slope. *A slide rule* = an instrument with two sliding pieces, used for making mathematical calculations. *A slide projector* = apparatus for showing photographic slides. *A hair slide* = a clip to keep women's hair tidy. *A landslide* = a large mass of rock and earth sliding down a hillside.

8 **a.** *A slap on the back* = a friendly informal greeting. *A thump* and *a punch* = *a blow* with the fist. *A poke* = a hard push with one finger. Only a slap is not painful here.

9 **a.** *Excursions* and *trips* are usually enjoyable one-day outings. We talk about *a journey* to work; *a voyage* of discovery, a sea voyage; a

scientific or military *expedition*; a holiday *tour*, a tour of inspection, a tour of duty.

10 **e.** *Custody* = safe, protective control. A *safety* officer makes sure that there is no danger to people; a *security* officer makes sure that property or secrets are not stolen. *Preservation* = keeping from decay or destruction (museums preserve old things; the preservation of your health, of peace). *To protect* = to guard from injury (sunglasses protect the eyes).

11 **a.** *Under lock and key* = (a fixed phrase) locked up. *A padlock* = a small, loose lock with a curved, hinged bar.

12 **a.** The proverb means that there are limits to what you can make someone do against his will. *To sip* = to drink, taking very small quantities at a time as with hot or strong drinks. *To imbibe* = (literary) to drink, take in (to imbibe beer, knowledge). *To swallow* = to send down the throat. *To quaff* = to drink deeply.

13 **b.** *A moving staircase = an escalator. A hoist* = a lifting device used by builders and on ships. *A conveyor belt* = a moving belt to carry heavy things, often used in factories.

14 **b.** All these are sharp points. Some flowers or bushes have *thorns*. Hooks and arrows have *barbs*, the backward pointing sharp part. Some fish have *spines*, as do porcupines. Goats, cows and snails have *horns*.

15 **a.** *Rigid* = very stiff. *Tense* = stiffened for the moment (to look tense, anxious). *Inflexible* = cannot be bent, resisting change (an inflexible person, rule). *Unbending* = unable to relax (a severe, unbending man).

16 **e.** *Petrified* = (literally) turned to stone. *Startled* and *alarmed* = rather frightened and disturbed. *Scared* = frightened. *Horrified* = very frightened and shocked.

17 **e.** *Sound in wind and limb* = completely healthy. *Something in the wind* = something about to happen. *To get your second wind* = to recover from initial tiredness, as in long distance running. *To get the wind up* = (slang) to become afraid. *To take the wind out of someone's sails* = to stop someone from acting or speaking by doing it first.

18 **b.** *For donkey's years* = for a very long time. *An ass* = a donkey. *A mare* = a female horse. *A pony* = a small horse for riding.

19 **e.** *Disloyalty* lets down friends and colleagues. *Infidelity* lets down a husband, wife or lover. *Treachery* betrays, and sometimes endangers friends and colleagues. *Falseness* = untruthfulness, disloyalty, deceit.

20 **c.** This is not correct English. *Absurdity* = silliness. All the others mean the same. *Nonsense* is the commonest word, *gibberish* the least common.

Unit ten

1 **c.** All these words mean equipment. Doctors and scientists use *instruments*. Fire fighters, gymnasts and chemists use *apparatus*. People use electrical *appliances* in the home (a hair dryer, a vacuum cleaner). Sailors, sportsmen and hunters use *gear*. Anglers and sailors use *tackle*.

2 **a.** *Illegible* = unreadable. All the others are wrong.

3 **e.** *A splint* = a piece of wood or metal to support something which is broken (to put a broken leg in a splint). *A sliver* = a very thin piece which has been cut off (a sliver of wood, meat). *A fragment* = a small piece which has broken off (a fragment of glass from a broken window). *A slice* = a piece (a slice of cake).

4 **a.** The correct phrase is: *the start of a journey*. All the others are common uses of *source*.

5 **d.** We write appointments or a record of what we have done in *a diary*. We usually keep photographs in *an album*. We look at the goods illustrated in *a catalogue* if we want to buy something. *A register* = a list of people's names kept as a record.

6 **d.** *A firebrand* = a public speaker who stirs up strong feelings. *A firelighter* = a device for lighting fires easily. *A fire fighter* = a fireman. *A fireplace* = the place in the house where we have a fire.

7 **c.** The proverb means we need occasional relaxation from work.

8 **b.** *A flash* = a sudden and brief show of bright light (a flash of lightning). *A glow* = a steady, warm light (red hot metal glows). *A gleam* = a ray of soft light that appears for a moment (the gleam of a lighthouse, the gleam of the sun in the early morning). *A flame* is rarely brief or we would call it a flare. *A blaze* = a fierce fire (to burst into a blaze; the blaze of the midday sun).

9 **b.** *To be joined in matrimony* = (a formal fixed phrase) to be married. All these words mean to join. We *fix* a cupboard on the wall with screws; we fix our eyes on a fascinating sight. We *attach* a label to a case with string. We *secure* a dog to a wall with a chain. We *fasten* papers together with a paper clip; we fasten a gate with a bolt.

10 **a.** *To duplicate* = to make an exact copy by machine (of written words). *To repeat, to echo* and *to reiterate* = to say again. *To imitate* = to copy and try to be like someone. If he was imitating writing we would say: He imitated my style.

11 **b.** Notice: *crisps* = (UK) potato crisps, (US) potato chips.
12 **c.** *A large piece of meat* could be a joint. All the others are different meanings of *block*.
13 **d.** (A fixed phrase.) Notice: *a split second* = a very short space of time (He reappeared in a split second).
14 **e.** *Wrinkles* = the lines on the skin which come with age. *A pleat* = a designed fold in cloth (pleats in a curtain, a skirt). *A fold* = a doubling back (a fold in a cloth, in the hills, in paper). *An overlap* = the place where one thing partly covers another (tiles on a roof overlap). *A crease* = a mark made by folding (a crease in paper, a crease down the front of trouser legs).
15 **b.** All these mean to get smaller. Dry wood *shrinks*. Metal *contracts* when it cools down. Speed and numbers *lessen*. Speed, numbers and time *decrease*. Sounds, money and hope *diminish*.
16 **b.** *To decline* = *to refuse* politely. *To reject* = to refuse. *To rebuff* and *to repulse* = to refuse someone in a very unfriendly way.
17 **e.** The *breaststroke* = a style of swimming, face downwards. *A stroke of luck* = a piece of luck. *Sunstroke* = illness resulting from the head being exposed to the sun. *The stroke of a pen* = one mark made by a pen (to correct a mistake with the stroke of a pen). *On the stroke* = exactly when the clock strikes (on the stroke of twelve).
18 **e**
19 **b.** A colloquial word, showing familiarity (a nice *bloke*, a funny bloke, a silly bloke).
20 **a.** *To ooze* = (of liquid) to appear very slowly (wet mud oozes; blood might ooze from a wound). *To pour* = to come in large quantities.

To gush = to come with a rush. *To spout* = to come fiercely, often rising upwards. *To trickle* = to come in a small stream.

Unit eleven

1 **e.** All these words mean to place. We *station* soldiers, guards etc. We *lodge* complaints, money with the bank. We *situate* someone in a comfortable job (uncommon). We *locate* a company's headquarters in London.

2 **a.** *Charitable* people help the poor in many ways. *Generous* people give things and help anyone readily. *Liberal* people provide things for others in generous quantities; also, liberal = open-minded, not prejudiced. *Hospitable* people entertain others freely in their homes. *Open-handed* people are generous.

3 **a.** *A crown* = (here) the highest point. The highest point of *a house* = the roof top. All the others are correct uses of crown. Notice: the crown of the *road* = the middle of the road which is higher than the side.

4 **d.** *Aristocrats* are said to have *blue blood*. *Once in a blue moon* = very rarely. *A bolt from the blue* = a sudden shock. *To scream blue murder* = to scream furiously. *A blue film* = an indecent film.

5 **b.** The idiom is always metaphorical.

6 **e**

7 **c.** *A tradition* = an old-established and cherished practice in a country, district or group of people (a family tradition). *A habit* = an established practice, often hard to break (smoking is a bad habit). *A practice* = something often repeated (to make a practice of getting up at 6 am). *Usage* = common practice (modern usage). *A routine* = a regular, sometimes boring, practice (a daily routine).

8 **e.** Vehicles *reverse*. Animals *rear* when they stand on their hind legs. Engines *backfire* when they explode through the exhaust pipe. *To return* = to come back.

9 **a.** *Cameras* and *eyes* have *a lens* to focus the light rays. Cameras and some *windows* have *shutters* to stop the light entering. We *load* a camera with a film. We can also load *ships* and *trains*.

10 **b.** Lions are supposed to be brave. Richard the Lion-heart was King Richard I (1157–99).

11 **a.** *Hollyhocks* can grow up to three metres high. They are common garden flowers.

12 **b.** We *grind* blades on a grindstone to sharpen them. *To pare* = to trim, to cut (to pare your nails, to pare the skin off an apple). *To shave* = to cut off hair or whiskers with a razor. *To file* = to use a file (to file your nails, to file through metal). *To scrape* = to rub or scratch with something sharp (to scrape paint off, to scrape the dirt off your shoes).

13 **e.** We do not describe people as *light* or *flimsy*. People are *weightless* in outer space. A *trivial* person has a shallow character.

14 **a.** Soldiers and *sailors* have *kitbags*. Walkers have *rucksacks*. *Haversacks* are smaller than rucksacks, but are also carried on the back. Schoolchildren carry *satchels*. *A carrier* = a paper shopping bag with string or plastic handles.

15 **e**

16 **b.** People who have lost an arm, leg, hand etc, often wear an *artificial* one. *Fake* = imitation (a fake picture). *A dummy* = an imitation for show only (a dummy gun made of wood). *Simulated* = pretended (simulated gold). *Mock* = not real (a mock battle, mock turtle soup).

17 **d.** The proverb means that money is responsible for producing all kinds of wickedness.

18 **a.** *Through thick and thin* = (a fixed phrase) through all troubles.

19 **d.** *To pass the time of day* = to greet. *To serve time* = to spend time in prison. *To keep time* = to keep in time with others, as in music. *To pass the time* = to do something to make the time go by. *To play for time* = to avoid making efforts until a certain time has arrived.

20 **c.** *A stench* = a bad *smell*. *An odour* = a smell. *A scent* and *an aroma* = a pleasant smell.

Unit twelve

1 **d.** *To rotate* = to go round and round (the earth rotates on its axis). *To roll* = to turn over and over (a ball rolls). *To revolve* = to turn in complete circles (wheels revolve). *To spin* = to turn round quickly (wheels spin). *To circulate* = to go in a circular path (blood circulates round the body).

2 **d.** *He imagined he was dead* = he thought he was dead. All the others mean that he made people think he was dead.

3 **b**

4 **e.** We talk about *a fit of anger*. *A dash of milk* = a small amount. *To cut a dash* = to look or act in a striking way. *A dashboard* = the instrument panel in a car. *A dash for shelter* = a quick, short run for shelter (from rain).

5 **a.** Also, *a muzzle* = a dog's nose and mouth. Notice: the muzzle of a rifle, but the *mouth* of a cannon. The *throat* = the passage at the back of the mouth. *An orifice* = an outside opening (e.g. a cave mouth).

6 **a**

7 **b.** *Antique* = old and valuable (antique furniture, pictures, but not people). *Aged* and *elderly* = old. *Venerable* = old and respected. *Senile* = old and weak in body and mind.

8 **e.** The proverb means that initial success is not necessarily the most valuable: only the final success counts.

9 **b.** *A sheaf* of corn = an armful of corn gathered and tied together. *A sheath* = a case in which a blade is kept (a sword in its sheath). *A stack* of corn can be as big as a house. *A bunch* of corn is unlikely unless the corn is for decoration like a bunch of flowers. *A clump* of corn = a small patch of growing corn.

10 **e.** *To give the password* = to identify yourself as a friend by saying a secret word. *A passing out parade* = a military parade at the end of a course. *To make a pass* = (colloquial) to make advances to a girl. *To pass along* = to move along. *To hold the pass* = to defend a narrow place and therefore stop an enemy's advance.

11 **c.** *Inattentive to the cost* is not English. We are inattentive when we do not listen (inattentive schoolboys). *Ignorant of the cost* = not knowing the cost. We are *insensible of* or *to* things when we do not notice them (insensible of the danger, insensible to the cold). *Unconscious of the cost* = unaware of the cost.

12 **d.** Notice also: chicken-hearted = cowardly.

13 **d.** *Agony* = very bad pain. *A twinge* = a slight, brief pain. *An ache* = a dull, continuous pain. You feel a *stinging* or *smarting* pain if you bathe a cut in your skin.

14 **a.** *To keep a straight face* = to show no emotion. *To pull a long face* = to look unhappy or disappointed. *To lose face* = to be humiliated, to lose one's reputation. *To have a face-lift* = to have cosmetic treatment to make the face look younger.

15 **a.** The *Cabinet* = the inner group of ministers in a government. *A constituency* = an area which elects a candidate. *A Whip* = (here) a Member

of Parliament who organises his colleagues when they vote.

16 **b.** Many desert people are *nomads*. *A pilgrim* = a religious person travelling to a holy place. *A vagrant* = someone with no home and no work. *An adventurer* = someone who uses rather dishonest ways to make a lot of money. *A tourist* = someone travelling for pleasure.

17 **e.** *Lethal* = deadly. *Mortal* = causing death (a mortal blow); also, lasting till death (this mortal life). *Fatal* = resulting in death (a fatal accident). *Homicidal* = to do with killing, murder (a homicidal maniac). *Killing* = (colloquial) very funny (a killing idea).

18 **c.** *A sovereign* = a ruler, a king. *Managers* and *supervisors* work in factories. Managers, *administrators*, *directors* and supervisors can work in offices.

19 **b.** (*Baked beans* are a cheap, popular food.) The others are all correct uses of *beam*. *Broad in the beam* = (slang) having wide hips.

20 **e.** None of the other answers is possible.

Unit thirteen

1 **a.** *Pointless* = without a purpose (a pointless question, activity).

2 **d.** The proverb means that if you are careful with all the small amounts of money you spend, you will always have plenty. We *look through* a telescope, a list of things, a book. We *look at* pictures, scenery. We *look up* a reference, a word in the dictionary; also, we look up an old friend when we visit him. We *look for* something we have lost.

3 **d.** A colloquial idiom.

4 **c.** *A key* = (here) the explanation at the bottom of a map of symbols used. *A scale* = (here) the

proportion between distances on the map and the actual distances (a scale of one kilometre to one centimetre). *A contour* = (here) a line on a map which joins all points at the same height.

5 **b**

6 **a.** Ladies wear *earrings* on their *ear lobes. An ear drop* = a hanging earring. *An earache* = a pain inside the ear. *An earphone* = an instrument, or part of an instrument (e.g. a telephone) you listen to.

7 **c.** Notice: *a ball* = *a dance.*

8 **c.** We *toss* a ball up, our hats in the air; we toss a coin. *To hurl* = to throw with all your strength. *To project* = to send forward. *To heave* = to lift and throw something heavy. *To propel* = to push forward.

9 **c.** We *distribute* gifts, prizes, notices. We *dispense* medicine and punishment. We *assign* jobs and seats. We *allot* work and money.

10 **b.** *Disasters* are always bad. The others can be good or bad things taking place.

11 **d.** *Panic* = complete unreasoning fear. *Timidity* = mild fear, shyness. *Fright* = fear. *Anxiety* = fear or uncertainty. *Concern* = worry.

12 **c.** *A sickle* = a curved hand tool, a reaping hook. *A scythe* = a large, two handed tool for cutting grass etc. *Shears* = a large scissor-like tool.

13 **d.** *A licence* = a paper granting permission for which one pays a fee (a television licence, a driving licence). *A charter* = official permission given by a ruler or government. *A permit* = an official paper allowing one to do something (an entrance permit). *A sanction* = official approval.

14 **e.** *To intrude* = to force your way in (Am I intruding?). *To insinuate* = to push your way in gradually (he insinuated himself into the

crowded room); also, to hint, to imply. *To inject* = to force into (to inject a painkilling drug). *To infiltrate* = to enter unnoticed (spies infiltrated the army).

15 **b.** All the others are wrong.

16 **d.** The nursery rhyme continues:

The cow jumped over the moon
The little dog laughed to see such sport
And the dish ran away with the spoon.

17 **e.** *To keep your balance* = not to fall over. *In the balance* = able to go one way or the other. *A balance wheel* = part of a watch or clock. *The balance of power* = the state of two unfriendly nations being equally strong. *To strike a balance* = to take a middle course, to make things even.

18 **b.** *A white elephant* = a possession that is a trouble to have, but cannot be given away. *The white of an egg* = the white part of the egg (as opposed to the yolk). *White horses* = the white tops of waves when the sea is rough. *A white feather* = a sign of cowardice (to show the white feather). *A white lie* = an unimportant untruth.

19 **a.** *An untruth* and *a falsehood* = a lie. *A forgery* = a copy made to trick other people. *A fib* = (childish) a lie. We tell untruths etc.; we do not *commit* them.

20 **d.** *String* is slack. *Pronunciation* is careless or sloppy. *A collar* is soft. *A seat* is soft.

Unit fourteen

1 **b.** *To conduct* = to lead (*an orchestral conductor*); also, to direct (*a lightning conductor*); also, to carry (*an electrical conductor*). A pipe to carry *water* = a conduit.

2 **c.** *A rafter* = a sloping wooden beam in a roof. The *eaves* = those parts of a roof which hang

over the walls. *A lintel* = the block of wood or stone over a door or window.

3 **d.** Before the days of computers, debits were printed in *red* on *bank accounts.*

4 **a.** *Public* = for use by anybody. *A public army* is nonsense, unless an army exists which any member of the public can rent. *Public conveniences* = public lavatories. In Britain *a public school* is not open to the public, but is a boarding school for selected, fee-paying pupils. *A public house* = a pub, where anyone may enter to drink.

5 **b.** *A rivet* = a metal pin which holds metal sheets together, as in ship-building.

6 **a.** *As thin as a rake* = (a fixed phrase) very thin. All these are tools. *A harrow* = a spiked framework which is dragged over the soil to break it up. *A trowel* = a small one-handed digging tool. *A fork* = (here) a garden fork, for digging. *A hoe* = a hand tool for breaking up the surface of the soil.

7 **d.** All are entrances, but *an inlet* = a place where the sea enters the land. *A threshold* = a stone or plank across the entrance to a building.

8 **a.** We inflate tyres with *a pump. A press* = printing machinery, or a device to press things (a clothes press). *An air gun* = a gun which uses compressed air. *A syringe* = a device for spraying or injecting liquid (a garden syringe, a hypodermic syringe). *A blower* = a machine which blows air.

9 **a.** Cars are not old enough to be *antiques. A veteran car* = one made before 1916. *A vintage car* = one made between 1916 and 1930. *Antiquated* = old and battered.

10 **a.** *Dismal* weather = dark, gloomy, miserable weather.

11 **e.** The proverb means that natural forces are stronger than any individual person. *A chap* and

a fellow = (colloquial) a man or boy. Notice: *a person* = any human being.

12 **c.** *Unlawful* = against the law (an unlawful act, an unlawful gathering). *Illegal* = not acceptable to the law (an illegal will, an illegal decision). *Prohibited* = forbidden (smoking prohibited). *Unauthorised* = without permission (an unauthorised sale, an unauthorised statement).

13 **a.** *By hook or by crook* = (a fixed phrase) by any way possible.

14 **b.** Pigeons *coo*, owls *hoot*, bees *drone* and lions *roar*.

15 **d.** *To hate* and *to detest* = to have a very strong *dislike*. *To abhor* and *to loathe* = to hate with disgust.

16 **a.** *To beat* is most likely, but *to overcome* is sometimes used. *To conquer* and *to vanquish* (old-fashioned) = to defeat an enemy. *To overthrow* = to bring to ruin (to overthrow a government, a ruler).

17 **b.** *Press-ups* = an athletic exercise for the arms and stomach muscles. *To press on* = to continue, to push forward. *Time presses* = there is no time to waste. *The press box* = seats reserved for journalists. *Press studs* = small, round fasteners that clip together (often on clothing).

18 **a**

19 **e.** *A forerunner* = something that appears in advance (dawn is the forerunner of day). *A header* = a dive; also, hitting a football with the head. *A precedent* = earlier action which encourages present action (a decision without precedent; to set a precedent). *A prefix* = a word or syllable placed in front of another word to change its meaning (post-war = after the war).

20 **d.** The *queen bee* = the only female bee that lays eggs within the swarm. *A hive* = a box in

which bees make their nest. *A cell* = (here) one of the wax compartments in a beehive in which the honey is stored; also, a compartment in a battery and a small room in a prison.

Unit fifteen

1 **e.** The nursery rhyme goes:

Jack and Jill went up the hill to fetch a pail of water
Jack fell down and broke his crown
And Jill came tumbling after.

2 **d.** *Mediocre* = second-rate and rather inferior. *Moderate, average* and *fair* = in the middle range. *Modest* = small but encouraging.

3 **b.** *A tanker* carries liquids, especially oil. *A coaster* = a small cargo-carrying boat which keeps near the coast. *A freighter* = a larger ocean-going cargo boat. *A trawler* catches fish with a large net, a trawl.

4 **c.** The phrase is colloquial and friendly. *A pew* = a long, wooden seat in a church.

5 **c.** *A hilt* = the handle of a sword or dagger.

6 **b.** *A filly* = a young female horse. *A gander* = a male goose. *A drake* = a male duck. *A stallion* = a male horse. *A ram* = a male sheep.

7 **b.** *A second* = (here) a boxer's assistant at a *boxing* match; also, 1/60 of a minute. *A ring* = (here) a square area where boxers fight; also, the circle of metal people wear on their fingers. *Break!* = (here) the order a referee gives to boxers to make them separate; we also talk about a break in the weather, when it changes.

8 **a.** Courts often impose *fines* for small offences. *A penalty* = a punishment for breaking a law (fines, imprisonment, death); or for breaking a rule in a game (a penalty kick in football). *A penance* = a self-punishment to show you are sorry (to give up drinking as penance for getting drunk). *A forfeit* = something you lose as a

punishment (My holiday was my forfeit for not working hard). *A confiscation* = something taken away as a punishment (the confiscation of someone's land).

9 **a.** *To run risks* = to take risks. We run into *danger,* we meet *perils,* we encounter *threats,* we find ourselves in *jeopardy.*

10 **e.** *A waste-paper basket = a litter basket. A rubbish tip* = a place where rubbish is piled up. *A refuse can* = (US) a rubbish bin.

11 **a.** The proverb means foolish men cannot look after their money.

12 **a.** *To pull someone round* = to help him to get better. *To pull someone to pieces* = to criticise him. *To pull your socks up* = (colloquial) to make efforts to improve. *To pull your weight* = to do your fair share of work. *To pull faces* = to make ugly faces as a sign of dislike or to be funny.

13 **c.** *Competitors* take part in a competition or race. *Applicants* apply for a job. *Claimants* make claims to own something. *Opponents* oppose each other in a game, sport or fight.

14 **b.** *Corridors* cannot be tight, though they may be narrow. *A tight shoe* is painful. *A tight string* is being pulled. *A tight corner* = a very sharp turning; also, (metaphorically) a dangerous position. *Tight-fisted* = unwilling to spend money.

15 **c.** *Modern* and *up-to-date* = new, of the present. *Novel* = new and attractive. *Fashionable* = in the fashion.

16 **a.** *A sudden sight of something* = a glimpse; also, we catch sight of something. The others are all meanings of *catch.*

17 **c.** A fixed phrase from the way animals fight.

18 **a.** *Pole-vaulting* = jumping with a pole. *Poles apart* = very different (often of people). *Up the pole* = (slang) crazy, mad. The *pole star* = the

North Star which shows true north. The *magnetic pole* = the point near the North Pole to which a compass needle points.

19 **d.** *Bus-driving* is an occupation. We spend years of training for *a profession*.

20 **d.** We *snip* with *scissors*, *saw* with a saw, *chop* with an axe, *carve* with a knife or a chisel and *slash* with a dagger or a sword.

Ihr Testergebnis

Unit one	☐	Unit nine	☐
Unit two	☐	Unit ten	☐
Unit three	☐	Unit eleven	☐
Unit four	☐	Unit twelve	☐
Unit five	☐	Unit thirteen	☐
Unit six	☐	Unit fourteen	☐
Unit seven	☐	Unit fifteen	☐
Unit eight	☐	GESAMT	☐

Wie geht es weiter?

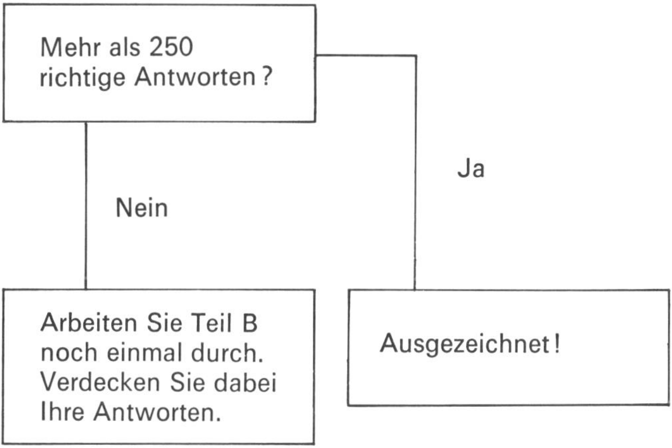

Inhalt